How to Give an Astrological Health Reading

A Step-by-step Approach to Giving
A Health Reading and
Determining Severity and Duration of Disease

Diane L. Cramer, M.S.

ISBN: 0-86690-332-1

First Printing: 1988
Second Printing: 1996

Cover Design: Phil Riske
Computer generated charts courtesy of Matrix Software Win☆Star

Published by:
American Federation of Astrologers, Inc.
PO Box 22040
6535 S. Rural Road
Tempe, AZ 85285-2040

Printed in the United States of America

Dedication

In memory of Charles Emerson

Acknowledgement

The author wishes to acknowledge the invaluable assistance
and encouragement of
Charles Emerson and Henry Niemann.
Though now deceased, their memory and work live on.

Contents

Foreword

When Bob Cooper sent me Diane Cramer's manuscript I was put into a bit of a dilemma. What was I, a physician, doing with a manuscript from a young lady who was not a physician and not even educated in a paramedical field?

I was positively impressed by the fact that she was a good, clear, concise writer and that despite her degrees in education, she had not fallen into the usual logorrheic jargon so common to the literature in this field.

Bob and Diane wanted my name mentioned as a technical consultant but I have been more like a technical editor. As the late F. Sims Pounds had written, only physicians should do medical astrology, but except for Margaret Millard and I there are no others in the free world, at least that I know about. During this entire century (excluding psychiatry) only five books have been written in English about medical astrology by physicians. From abroad there has been only the work of Eugene Jonas and associates, primarily on astrological birth control, written about by Ostrander and Schroeder. It has, therefore, been incumbent on astrologers other than physicians to fill in the void in the literature.

This book is unique in that it is for the beginner. I have been pleased to give a little aid in finalizing the manuscript.

Harry F. Darling, M.D., PMAFA
1988

Introduction to Revised Edition

Since the publication of this book in 1988, there has been a growing awareness of health, healing, and ways to improve one's diet. Many persons undergoing a health crisis are choosing alternative forms of healing rather than turning to traditional medicine. To some extent, the results of some alternative forms of healing are more anecdotal than scientifically based.

Similarly, medical astrology could be considered an alternative form of healing - useful for preventive and informational purposes. But unlike other alternative healing methods, medical astrology seems to be in a league all its own. There are still not that many medical astrology books, astrologers proficient in medical astrology, nor persons willing to use medical astrology as an aid to improving health. So, despite the author's increased knowledge since the 1988 publication, it does not appear that medical astrology has made much of an impact on the general public over the past eight years.

One should not forget that medical astrology was used by the ancients so it is certainly not a new subject. However, for those of you interested in medical astrology, while you are educating yourself on the subject it will be necessary to educate those with whom you come into contact about what medical astrology is and what it can and cannot do.

This revised edition of *How to Give An Astrological Health Reading* contains much of the same information as the first edition since over the past eight years the author has found the information in the first edition to be reliable in the study of medical astrology. The revised edition has two new case studies—an astrological analysis of a man with Lou Gehrig's Disease and an astrological analysis of a woman who received a liver transplant. Plus, there is an additional chapter on homeopathy and its use and on the twelve tissue salts corresponding to the twelve signs of the zodiac. Other small additions have been made throughout the book such as additional significators of disease, and more information on the signs and planets.

During the past eight years, the author has continued to counsel clients using medical astrology and still believes what was stated in the first edition—that medical astrology cannot be used to diagnose illness, that it may be able to confirm the seriousness of a disease, that nutritional information can be found in the birth chart, and that one is able to see one's strengths and weaknesses in the birth chart. If there were one area the author could concentrate on over the next eight years, it would be the use of the elements fire, earth, air, and water in analyzing health lacks and needs, especially in terms of nutritional needs. Otherwise, proficiency for the author and the student continues to be in analyzing as many types of charts as possible in terms of health. Perhaps at some point in the future there will be a definite genetic or astrological method to pinpoint potential medical problems. Astrologically, this would require hundreds of charts with a common problem to see if there is a disease signature that can be isolated. One could then advise on lifestyle changes based on the natal chart.

Introduction

In recent years has come the recognition of the value of the natal birth chart in assessing general health. An analysis of the natal chart can explain, for example, why some people can smoke cigarettes without developing lung disease, while others have the potential for developing lung disease from cigarettes due to the presence in the natal chart of certain astrological disease indicators for lung disease.

Giving a health reading places a great responsibility on the astrologer, for in a health reading we could plant seeds for an illness instead of giving a client vital information from the chart to help to maximize health and help prevent future illnesses. The same ethical standards that all astrologers should abide by in giving general readings should be honored.

A medical astrologer should be experienced in chart interpretation and predictive techniques. A medical astrologer should also be well versed in medical terminology and nutrition. A knowledge of anatomy and physiology will help in correlating bodily action and location of potential problems. Although some physicians are also medical astrologers, the medical astrologer is usually not a physician so need not worry about having the knowledge of an M.D. But we must point out to our clients what possible health problems exist so that they can have tests or diagnoses made by a physician. *It is against the law for a medical astrologer who is not also a physician to diagnose and treat a condition.* The medical astrologer can only point out the chart indications and recommend the type of medical practitioner who might be helpful to the client.

Like all areas of astrology, a medical reading has its limitations. The chart should be used as an adjunct with other methods of health assessment. The chart can be helpful in pointing out bodily strengths and weaknesses and can often point out severity and duration of a particular health problem. However, there can be gray areas where the exact nature of a condition is not known.

The author has found three reasons to analyze a chart in terms of health. In the first instance, the medical astrologer is asked to give a health reading—to judge the natal chart in terms of health. The medical astrologer can indicate the client's natural immunities, possible disease indicators, weak points in the body and nutritional deficiencies. In the second instance the medical astrologer may be called upon to interpret the chart of a person with a serious illness or health disorder so as to furnish extra information to aid in determining severity and duration of the condition. In the third instance the medical astrologer may be asked to determine what astrological indicators are shown—using natal chart techniques and predictive techniques—to explain an illness that traditional medicine has been unable to diagnose or cure.

This book is a step-by-step approach of procedures to use in assessing health. By following a specified format each time a medical reading is done, one will be able to learn the techniques of medical astrology as well as have an organized format of information. This book should be used primarily as a tool in practicing "preventive medicine." The author is not responsible for misuse of the book by someone not licensed to practice medicine. Again, the medical astrologer should not attempt to diagnose or cure a client but must refer the client to a licensed physician.

There are many excellent books on the market to assist the medical astrologer in giving a health reading. This "how-to" book will give assistance in utilizing these books to facilitate a health reading. The end of the book lists a bibliography of books the author has found useful in assessing health. Also included is a glossary of medical terms. Footnotes for information cited are also listed.

Chapter One

Signs and Planets in Medical Astrology

An understanding of the meaning of the signs and planets as used in medical astrology is necessary before proceeding to the steps to a medical chart analysis. Most medical astrology books list what the author feels is the proper rulership for each of the planets and signs of the zodiac. *Davidson's Medical Astrology*, *The American Book of Nutrition and Medical Astrology*, *Essentials of Medical Astrology* and *Mind and Body in Astrology* have sophisticated approaches to rulership.

Generally speaking, the signs of the zodiac refer to the anatomical locations in the body while the planets refer to the physiology and function of an organ or tissue. Some authors of medical astrology books give planetary rulership to the various organs in the body. But the planets describe the action or non-action of an organ while the signs of the zodiac refer to the anatomical location. The signs can be descriptive of bodily action as well as identifying bodily location.

Note the ability of Taurus to aggregate, Scorpio to eliminate, Aries to excite, etc. But again, it is the influence of a planet—either by tenancy or afflicting the ruler of a sign—that influences the action of the signs. Saturn afflicting Mercury or in Gemini can disturb respiration. Mars afflicting Mercury or in Gemini can inflame the lungs. The use of planetary rulerships in medical astrology—including the old rulerships of Mars for Scorpio, Saturn for Aquarius and Jupiter for Pisces is valid. It should be noted that no matter how many medical astrology books one reads, there is never total agreement on this question of rulership.

Sign Rulerships

The following discussion of rulerships is presented as a guide. It is a summary of information gleaned from several medical astrology books and the results of the author's study of anatomy and physiology correlated with the essential nature of the signs and planets. The information should not be taken as cold, hard fact but should be considered a possible working mode.

Notice also that one organ can be ruled by more than one sign depending on which of its functions is being described. In *Essentials of Medical Astrology*, Harry F. Darling, M.D. states that "positive signs correspond with the tissues which have to do with fight/flight, and the negative ones with those tissues which sustain and nourish the organism.[1]

Aries

Aries is descriptive of heat, inflammation and energy. As the first sign of the zodiac, it rules the head including the skull and face. It rules the outer ears, the eyeballs, the brain, the upper jaw, the adrenal medulla and pituitary gland. Due to its polarity with Libra, it is associated with renal functions.

Taurus

Taurus, which refers to the senses, is a sign that takes in as opposed to its opposite—Scorpio—which eliminates. As an aggregator, it can be involved in tumor formation. It is a sign that can aid in the support and endurance of the body. It rules the gums, Islets of Langerhans, tonsils, throat, vocal cords, salivary glands, adenoids, pharynx, larynx, the iris, middle ear, lower jaw, and palate. It appears to rule the thyroid gland and thymus gland.

Gemini

Gemini can be descriptive of restlessness and nervousness. Gemini is associated with flexibility, dispersal, communication and connectivity. It rules the tubes of the body. It has rulership over the lungs (inhalation), the central nervous system, the shoulders, arms, hands, eustachian tubes of the ears, the neck, trachea, ureter, urethra, fallopian tube, vas deferens, the bronchi and the tongue. It rules capillaries and collagen.

Cancer

Cancer, which is moist, can be fluctuating but tenacious. It is a sign of nurturing and protectiveness. It rules all coverings and containers in the body. It rules mucous membranes, the sinus cavities, cheeks of the face, bone marrow, the stomach, chest cavity, the uterus, pleura, body fluids, the endocardium, pericardium, meninges, the glycogen storage of the liver, the spleen in its storage capacity and the posterior pituitary gland. It also rules the breasts, eye sockets and the abdominal sac—the peritoneum. It rules chymification—gastric digestion and probably rules the rib cage in its role of protection. Cancer, rather than Capricorn, most likely rules the gallbladder since it is principally an organ of storage while Capricorn could rule gallstones.

Leo

Leo is a sign of energy and vitality. It rules the muscular portion of the heart, the sternum, the spine and middle back. It is thought to rule the superior and inferior vena cava and the aorta, coronary arteries and the pulmonary artery.

Virgo

Virgo, which can indicate nervousness, rules the processes of assimilation, selection and utilization in the body. It rules the process of discrimination and is involved in splitting and separating. It rules the small intestine, the pancreas, duodenum, and the enzyme production of the liver. It rules chylification or primary assimilation and rules amino acid formation in the intestines.

Libra

Libra refers to the principle of balance and the processes of filtration and distillation. It rules the vasomotor system, the lower back (lumbar region), the glandular vascular part of the kidney and the skin as it relates cosmetically.

Scorpio

Scorpio, a sign of elimination, rules bodily outlets and procreative processes. It has the ability to throw off and readapt itself. It rules the colon, bladder, the ovaries, the mucous membranes of the nose, the large intestine, rectum, vagina, testes and prostate gland. It also rules the pelvis of the kidney.

Sagittarius

Sagittarius can refer to locomotion and transference. It rules the exhalation process of the lungs, the hips and thighs, ilium, femur, sacrum, sciatic nerve, saphenous vein and the ischium. Its rulership of the liver appears to be the involvement of the liver in fat storage and utilization. The liver is also the largest inner organ in the body.

Capricorn

Capricorn can be cold and dry. It refers to limitation and the process of hardening. It rules the skin in its role of protector and also rules the knees, hair, bones, nails, teeth and cell walls. It is said to rule the anterior pituitary gland.

Aquarius

Aquarius can refer to rare illnesses and nervous ailments. It is involved in blood circulation and the oxidation processes in the body. It rules the lower leg, calf and ankles, valves of the heart, the cornea and retina. It may rule the parathyroid glands.

Pisces

Pisces can refer to weird ailments such as diseases that are hard to diagnose or cure, diseases of mental origin or a disease discovered in an advanced stage without prior symptoms. Pisces can refer to incurable diseases. It can have a relaxing and softening effect and is involved in the production of phlegm and mucus. It rules the feet and toes, the lymphatic system, and the spleen in its lymphatic role. It may also be involved with the lungs and the pineal gland.

Of great importance are the polarities between signs. An affliction in Aries can indicate a medical problem in a Libra ruled organ or tissue and vice versa. And going a step further, an affliction in any one or more signs of a quadruplicity can indicate a medical problem in any one of the four signs. Thus, an affliction in Taurus could manifest in a Taurus-related organ or in one ruled by Scorpio, Leo, or Aquarius. There are cardinal, fixed and mutable types of illnesses. Step Four in Chapter Two will explain how to determine what, if any, quadruplicities are afflicted—either through tenancy by a malefic or by afflictions to the ruler of a sign.

Signs in Relation to Illness

Following is a list of diseases associated with each sign according to quadruplicity. This list can be used as a guide as to possible manifestations of afflictions in a sign.

Diseases Associated with Each Sign

Cardinal

Aries: Cerebral congestion, headaches, migraine, stroke, delirium, vertigo, high fever, head accident, eye problems, brain damage, concussion, pimples.

Cancer: Digestive troubles, stomach complaints, anemia, hiccups, water retention, flatulency, disease caused by wrong diet, breast cancer, nausea, vomiting, peptic ulcer, pericarditis, endocarditis, chest constriction.

Libra: Nephritis, Bright's disease, headaches, skin rashes, blood disorders, lumbago, suppression of urine, kidney ailments.

Capricorn: Falls, bruises, dislocation of bone, rheumatism, hives, colds and chills, arthritis, weak knees, skin disease, bone disease, deafness, dental problems, leprosy, stiff joints.

Fixed

Taurus: Earache, sore throat, swollen glands, suffocation, mumps, tumors, abscesses, thyroid problems, gingivitis, laryngitis, strangulation, tonsillitis, gum disease.

Leo: Fevers, spinal meningitis, sunstroke, middle back pains, spinal trouble, myocarditis, cardiomyopathy, myocardial infarction, angina, anemia.

Scorpio: Ruptures, hernia, fistula, piles, venereal disease, menstrual irregularities, disease of the generative organs, prostrate trouble, kidney stones, retention of urine, hemorrhoids, nasal catarrh.

Aquarius: Sprained or broken ankle, impurities of bloodstream, circulatory problems, leg cramps, varicose veins, nervous disease, swelling of legs, blood poisoning, incomplete oxygenation, heart palpitation, heart arrhythmia.

Mutable

Gemini: Asthma, lung disorders, bronchitis, pneumonia, pleurisy, anxiety, mental overtrain, hysteria, nervous diseases, neuralgia, respiratory problems, speech defect, emphysema.

Virgo: Intestinal disorders, duodenitis, diarrhea, dysentery, malnutrition, peritonitis, worms, appendicitis, colic, nervous disorders.

Sagittarius: Rheumatism, gout, hip injuries, sciatica, hip disease, cirrhosis of the liver, obesity, jaundice.

Pisces: Bunions, gout, tumors, swelling of feet, deformed feet, virus infections, mucus discharge, lung disease, alcoholism, psychosomatic illnesses, flat feet.

The list is not all-inclusive as most diseases will be seen as part of a larger configuration of signs and planets. Note that Daath gives falls or injuries from horses and gunshot wounds to Sagittarius.[2]

Planetary Actions and Reactions to Disease

The planets determine action or reaction to disease according to the nature of the planet and its inter-aspects. The site of the disease is determined by quadruplicity. States Heinrich Daath in *Medical Astrology*:

"Each planetary body may be said to function in three different ways...In an individual's nativity, there may be too much of some particular planet's energy, an insufficiency or a permutation... Each planet imparts a special type of disease to an organ, but becomes modified, changed or disguised by reception of cross aspects from other planets. From the combination of planet, sign, aspect and house we may infer structural and functional disorder."[3]

Planets receiving hard aspects can result in various health disorders. For example, there is a similarity in the effects of afflictions to either the Sun or Mars in that both can be indicative of a high fever, an infection, inflammation or energy problems. However, Mars is more involved in pain and muscular disorders than the Sun. And though both Mars and Pluto are indicative of infection and inflammation, Pluto is considered more powerful in its effects, causing massive infections. Mars may relate to a twenty-four hour virus whereas Pluto relates to infections lasting weeks or months.

The Moon and Mercury can both contribute to nervous or mental disorders, but the Moon relates more to disturbances in bodily cycles while Mercury, in affliction, affects the nervous or respiratory systems.

Mars and Saturn can be thought of as opposites in their effects—Mars being hot and Saturn being cold—Mars indicating acidity and Saturn indicating alkalinity. Mars is acute in its effects whereas Saturn can be chronic.

Neptune appears to be the most insidious in its effects as one may not be aware of a disease until it has progressed way beyond its initial beginning. There is also the potential for misdiagnosis and adverse reaction to drugs with Neptune.

The following can be used as a guide to determine possible planetary actions and reactions to disease:

Determining Possible Planetary Actions and Reactions to Disease

Sun: Inflammation, infection, fever, energy problems, heart disorder, cell vitality.

Moon: Inconstancy, emotional disorder, water retention, allergic reactions, bodily secretions, mucous formation, altered body rhythm, acute ailments, disturbances in bodily cycles, psychological problems, fluid balance.

Mercury: Mental disorders, disturbance in mental health, respiratory disorders, nervous disorders, altered cell communication, hormonal imbalance, speech disorders.

Venus: Imbalance of bodily energies, benign growths, blood sugar imbalance, reduced input of sensory organs, problems with venous circulation, lack of tone.

Mars: Inflammation, infection, acute disease, fever, eruptive action, blood ailments, bruises, wounds, acidosis, burns, irritation, ulcers, flare-ups, surgery, sudden illness, pain, muscular disorders, hemorrhages.

Mars can indicate, by sign or quadruplicity, an overworked part of the body where one may be more subject to infection or acute flare-ups.

Jupiter: Problems with arterial blood circulation, enlarged organ, disease caused by excess, disposition of bodily fat, problem with fat assimilation, swellings, engorgement, obesity, faulty condition of blood, lung hemorrhage.

In good aspect Jupiter will aid to preserve life. By sign tenancy it can indicate an enlarged organ; by planetary function it indicates expansion—positively or negatively depending on aspects. Its malignant effects can be seen in its old rulership of Pisces, which rules the immune system.

Saturn: Chronic disease, alkalinity, hardening, cold, retention, crystallization, calcification, obstruction, malnutrition, uric acid deposits, malignancy, atrophy, skin disease, hair loss, underactivity.

By sign tenancy, Saturn can indicate an underdeveloped or small organ. It can indicate a weak point in the body where one is more prone to disease, a weak area exacerbated by stress. There is less of a blood supply to that organ. Attention should be given to that part of the body. For example, Saturn in Leo can indicate a weak heart muscle which can be strengthened by exercise. Saturn in Gemini can indicate weak lungs—avoid smoking. Note also polarity and quadruplicity where Saturn is concerned.

Uranus: Incoordination, spasm, sudden illness, cramps, convulsions, ruptures, seizures, twitching, restlessness, stress-related ailments, heart palpitations, epilepsy, accidents caused by electricity or explosion, nervousness.

Neptune: Bodily weakness, drug addiction, alcoholism, hallucinations, coma, poison, malignancy, hidden illness, overdose, delusions, drug sensitivity, lowered immune system, misdiagnosis, consequence of abuse of stimulants

Pluto: Hereditary diseases, malformation, malignancy, cell replication, massive infections, inflammation, bacterial infections, amputation

Information on an actual disorder can be inferred by combining keywords such as Mercury-Venus for sensory nerves and Mercury-Mars for motor nerves. *Medical Astrology* (Nauman), *Complete Astro-Medical Index* and *A Handbook of Medical Astrology* contain sections on planetary aspects in medical astrology.

Planets are caused to act or react based on their essential natures of hot, cold, dry, wet and humid as these properties combine in aspect combination. For those who wish to investigate this complex subject they are referred to the following two books: *Medical Astrology* by Heinrich Daath and *Cornerstones of Astrology* by Friedrich "Sinbad" Schwickert and Adolf Weiss.

Aspects in Medical Astrology

Mention should be made of the use and definition of aspects particular to medical astrology. As in other areas of astrology, aspects are classified as hard and soft. The hard aspects used throughout this book are the semisextile, square, semisquare, sesquiquadrate, quincunx and opposition. The soft aspects are the trine and the sextile. The semisextile is considered a hard aspect since its effects are similar to the quincunx in that inharmonious signs are brought into play. The conjunction is the strongest aspect in its effects on health and is interpreted (and determined to be a hard or soft aspect) according to the nature of the planets involved. However, all the aspects have an effect on health interpretation based on the general rule that aspects involving the personal points of the chart—the Sun, Moon and the angles (Ascendant, Descendant, Midheaven, Imum Coeli, Vertex, Antivertex)—will demonstrate the strongest

6

effects on health—for better or worse—with the conjunction being the strongest aspect. Soft aspects in general do not indicate a health condition but usually describe an area of strength in the body. Hard aspects between planets and personal points can describe a propensity toward a particular health condition based on the nature of the signs and planets involved. In predictive techniques, soft aspects can indicate an easing of a health condition; hard aspects can indicate a crises situation or a worsening of a health condition (see Chapter Three, Assessing Severity and Duration of Disease).

Aspect strength can also be determined by the orb of influence between the planets and/or angles involved. As a rule, orbs of major aspects should not exceed seven and one half degrees. And the closer an aspect is to exactness, the more obvious and stronger will be its effects. The following table is a guide to determine the orbs of influence that can be used for aspects when interpreting a natal chart for health. One may be justified at times in using larger orbs than those stated (such as aspects involving personal points), and it is at those times that one's intuition must be used.

A Guide to Determining Orbs of Influence

Aspect		Orb of Influence
Conjunction	0-7°30'	7°30'
Semisextile	30°	2°
Semisquare	45°	3°
Sextile	60°	4°
Square	90°	7°
Trine	120°	7°
Sesquiquadrate	135°	4°
Quincunx	150°	4°
Opposition	180°	7°30'

It should be noted that when utilizing predictive techniques, a major health crisis can be touched off by a transit or an eclipse to a planet or angle that is close to exactitude in degrees and minutes. The above table is best utilized in natal chart interpretation.

In analyzing any chart, the parallels of declination should also be listed as they are also planets and/or angles in aspect to each other and can add additional information to the chart interpretation.

The parallels of declination are the positions of the planets north or south of the celestial equator. If one is calculating a chart by hand, the parallels can be derived from any ephemeris that lists declinations. The same mathematical formula used in finding the motion of the planets is used to find the motion of the planets in declination. The declination of the Ascendant can be found by looking in the ephemeris for the day the Sun is in the same degree and minute as the Ascendant. For example, taking an Ascendant of 25 Virgo using a midnight ephemeris, one would look for the date the Sun is at 25 Virgo (September 19) and look at the declination of the Sun on September 19, which is 1N44. The declination of the Ascendant would be found by finding the motion between September 19 and 20. The same procedure is applied in finding the declination of the Midheaven. After listing all the parallels of declination, one should note whether the parallels are in aspect to each other. Using an orb of one degree, planets or personal points both north or both south of the celestial equator are considered parallel to each other; with one planet north and the other south of the celestial equator, (with a one degree orb), the aspect is called a contraparallel. There is no real agreement among astrologers on the interpretation of parallels—most feel parallels work like conjunctions and contraparallels work like oppositions. In *Planetary Pictures In Declination*, however, Roger Hutcheon makes a good case for interpreting both parallels and contraparallels as conjunctions working on a subliminal level.[4] In any event, they should not be overlooked when examining the natal chart as planets in aspect in both longitude and declination are stronger than either one alone. By checking parallels, one may discover subtle influences affecting the physical body.

A chart analysis would not be complete without a listing and interpretation of relevant midpoints. Midpoints are located halfway between two planets and/or angles. Because there are two such halfway points, measuring clockwise and counterclockwise in the horoscope, one exactly opposite the other, each midpoint is duplex.

Midpoints are commonly expressed by using a slash between the planets and/or angles from which they are derived. For example in the chart analysis of Figure II, the midpoint of Mercury and Neptune is at 12 Aries/Libra 04. This is expressed as Mercury/Neptune 12 Aries/Libra 04.

When a planet is at a midpoint—conjunct one dual point and in opposition to the other—the equal sign may be used to express this relationship. In the example above, the Sun at 11 Libra 04 is at Mercury/Neptune. This is expressed: Sun ll Libra 04 = Mercury/Neptune 12 Aries/Libra 04.

When a planet is square the (duplex) midpoint, the word "square" is used instead of the equal sign; if written rather than typed, the symbol for square is used. There are also semisquare/sesquiquadrate relationships which may be expressed in the same manner as is the square.

In some subspecialized systems of astrology, especially Cosmobiology, only one of the paired aspects is used. In these systems midpoints are also referred to as half-sums.

Students can learn more about midpoints in such books as *Applied Cosmobiology* by Reinhold Ebertin or *Cosmobiology: A Modern Approach to Astrology* by Doris E. Greaves. The strongest midpoint configuration is a conjunction or opposition involving a personal point in the chart—the Sun, Moon, Ascendant, or Midheaven. The orb of influence for midpoint structures generally should not exceed one and a half degrees. However, there will be instances in this book when orbs of up to two degrees have been used as the midpoint interpretation was found to be more than a coincidence. One may find interpretations for midpoint structures relating to health in *The Combination of Stellar Influences* by Reinhold Ebertin, *Astrological Healing* by Reinhold Ebertin; *Midpoints Unleashing the Power of the Planets* by Michael Munkasey, *Medical Astrology* by Eileen Nauman, and/or *Astrology Key to Holistic Health* by Marcia Starck.

The arithmetical calculation of midpoints is laborious, especially if all of them are calculated to the minute. This labor may be saved by means of the computer. If you have no computer, the ninety degree wheel is very useful. See Footnotes 44 and 45 for information on ordering midpoint structures.

Chapter Two

Steps to Giving A General Health Reading

The approach that follows utilizes traditional methods of astrology. All charts illustrated in this book are tropical/Placidus. Before assessing a chart it is helpful to have the client fill out a questionnaire describing his or her past medical history. This aids in confirming natal chart tendencies. A medical questionnaire and directions for its use can be found in *Medical Astrology* by Eileen Nauman.

A medical chart evaluation begins with an investigation of the Sun, Moon and Ascendant.

Step One—Analyzing the Sun

The Sun is descriptive of the constitution and vitality and can be an indicator of one's ability to withstand disease. A prominent Sun receiving good aspects can indicate a strong constitution and good vitality. A weakly placed Sun (by house or sign) or one receiving many hard aspects can cause energy problems and difficulty in withstanding disease.

Doris Chase Doane conducted a longevity study using 150 timed birthcharts of people who lived more than 70 years. The results indicated that for longevity the best aspect was Mars to the Sun and the best position is the Sun on an angle. She found that any aspect between Mars and the Sun or between Jupiter and the Sun indicates vitality. However, a badly afflicted Mars could shorten life due to infection or accident.[5]

The Sun should be examined as to sign and house position. Generally, the Sun is considered strongest by sign in fire, followed by air, water and earth. This can be modified for better or worse by house position and aspects. For example, an angular Sun in a water or earth sign receiving no hard aspects would be considered stronger, with a greater ability to resist disease, than the Sun in a fire or air sign and posited in a cadent house and afflicted by outer planets. *Davidson's Medical Astrology* describes Capricorn as not robust but tending toward longevity. Cancer has great tenacity and Taurus has "great natural strength if it will avoid toxicity."[6]

The aspects to the Sun should be examined next. The hard aspects to the Sun can have an effect on health. The following is a brief guide to interpreting hard aspects to the Sun.

A Guide to Interpreting Hard Aspects to the Sun

Sun-Moon: Affects vitality, emotional imbalance, eye problems.

Sun-Mercury: Affects nerves, respiration, hormonal imbalance.

Sun-Venus: Alters equilibrium, swollen glands, self-indulgence.

Sun-Mars: May result in acute infection, fever, burns, accident, acidosis, muscular disorders.

Sun-Jupiter: Can indicate sickness due to excess.

Sun-Saturn: Possibility of chronic disease, depletion of energy, poor appetite, alkalinity, rheumatism, arteriosclerosis.

Sun-Uranus: Erratic energy level, nervous disorder, circulatory problems, paralysis.

Sun-Neptune: Lowered resistance, depleted energy, lack of tone, misdiagnosis of illness, edema, eye disease.

Sun-Pluto: Altered recuperative ability, massive infections, stress-related illness.

Soft aspects to the Sun (sextile or trine) indicate an easy flow of energy between the Sun and the planet aspecting it. Thus the Sun in harmony with the Moon would aid emotional balance and vitality. In harmony with Mercury, the nervous system is strengthened, in harmony with Venus, bodily energies are balanced, in harmony with Mars or Jupiter there is healthy blood, vitality and resistance to disease, in harmony with Saturn, there is endurance. In harmony with Uranus there is energy and improved circulation. Neptune in harmony with the Sun adds a benign influence and Pluto in harmony with the Sun aids recuperative powers and adds toughness to the constitution.

More information about the Sun can be gained by examining any parallels to the Sun (see discussion of parallels in Aspects in Medical Astrology, Chapter One). By checking parallels to the Sun, one can find more influences affecting the physical body.

To complete the analysis of the Sun, midpoints to it should be checked (see discussion of midpoints in Aspects in Medical Astrology, Chapter One). Midpoints provide additional information on the cosmic state of a planet.

Step Two—Analyzing the Moon

After analyzing the Sun, the next step is to analyze the Moon to determine the conditions of health. According to some medical astrologers, a well-aspected Moon indicates good health, even if the Sun shows poor vitality. You may not be physically strong, but you will rarely become ill. Conversely, one with a well-aspected Sun but a poorly aspected Moon is physically strong, but will be ill from time to time. Since the author has seen charts of persons with well aspected Moons who contracted serious illnesses, one cannot always assume that a well-aspected Moon describes a person rarely ill. One may assume, however, that a poorly aspected Moon does describe a person who may be ill from time to time. The Moon is best analyzed in terms of emotional needs, habits and bodily rhythms which can affect health. A repression of emotional needs or a disturbance of the bodily rhythms can be a causative factor in illness.

One should note the hard aspects to the Moon both in longitude and in declination. The following can be used as a guide in evaluating the Moon in hard aspect.

A Guide to Evaluating the Moon in Hard Aspect

Sun-Moon: Conflict between emotions and will, bodily rhythms altered, energy fluctuation, fluid imbalance.

Moon-Mercury: Oversensitivity, nervousness, worry.

Moon-Venus: Difficulty in emotional satisfaction, bodily rhythms altered, water imbalance, PMS in females.

Moon-Mars: Overanxious, overreacts emotionally, hyper, acid stomach.

Moon-Jupiter: Excessive emotionality, overindulgent, difficulty in fat assimilation, digestive disorders.

Moon-Saturn: Emotional repression, anxious, difficulty in self-expression, defect of mucous membranes.

Moon-Uranus: Erratic behavior, overreacts, emotional tension, nervous, willful.

Moon-Neptune: Fearful, escapist tendencies (drugs, alcohol food, TV), water imbalance, unusual cravings, allergies.

Moon-Pluto: Obsessive, extremist, altered bodily rhythms, mood swings, fibroid tumors.

The Moon afflicted in the signs can indicate the following emotional conditions or habits which can lead to a physical or mental health disorder.

A Guide to Emotional Considerations or Habits

Moon in Aries: Overemotional, high-strung, tense, reckless.

Moon in Taurus: Overindulgent in food or drink, rigid disposition.

Moon in Gemini: Nervousness, instability, anxious.

Moon in Cancer: Emotional stress, fluctuating emotions.

Moon in Leo: Overestimation of self.

Moon in Virgo: Worry, anxiety, nervousness.

Moon in Libra: Overindulgence, emotional imbalance.

Moon in Scorpio: Overestimating self, overemotional.

Moon in Sagittarius: Nervousness, overindulgence.

Moon in Capricorn: Emotional repression, rigidity.

Moon in Aquarius: Erratic emotions, nervousness.

Moon in Pisces: Escapism, moodiness, inferiority complex, vagueness.

Midpoints involving the Moon should be examined next. A synthesis of the Moon in aspect, sign, and midpoint configuration will give indications of emotional stability, self-expression, and habit patterns.

Step Three—Analyzing the Ascendant

The Ascendant represents the physical body. It may also describe the birth process. According to Davidson's *Medical Astrology*, the Ascendant represents "the kind of conductivity or resistance, which the physical body offers."[7] Fire and air signs rising are good conductors of energy with water and earth being more resistant. Aspects to the Ascendant can alter the flow of energy throughout the body, positively or negatively depending on the planet. The following is a brief description of possible effects of planets in hard aspect to the Ascendant.

Effects of Planets in Hard Aspect to the Ascendant

Sun-Ascendant: Fevers, depletion of energy, eye trouble.

Moon-Ascendant: Inconstant flow of energy, functional disorders, lack of objectivity, PMS in females, watery birth.

Mercury-Ascendant: Worry, nervous disorders, respiratory ailments.

Venus-Ascendant: Overindulgence, throat and kidney ailments.

Mars-Ascendant: Fevers, inflammation, muscular disorders, bruises, accidents, infections, surgical operations, use of forceps at birth.

Jupiter-Ascendant: Weight gain, overindulgence, blood disorder.

Saturn-Ascendant: Hindered flow of energy, chronic health problems, skin disorders, difficult labor.

Uranus-Ascendant: Erratic flow of energy, nervousness, circulatory ailments, headaches.

Neptune-Ascendant: Depletion of energy; lowered immunity; infection; dependency on alcohol, drugs, coffee or tea; effects of alcohol or smoking by the mother.

Pluto-Ascendant: Inflammation, physical change, hereditary disorders, force at birth—Caesarian section, forceps, forced birth.

Node-Ascendant: Hospital birth.

The Sun, Mars or Pluto rising can aid the flow of energy throughout the body despite a weak rising sign or hard aspects to the Ascendant.

Step Four—Determining Quadruplicity Emphasis

The quadruplicities are used in medical astrology to determine the type and severity of disease as shown in the natal chart. There are two ways this can be done—either through a point system or by examining actual quadruplicities. In the first instance one examines the placement of planets in signs to determine whether one quadruplicity predominates over the others. The cardinal signs are Aries, Cancer, Libra and Capricorn. The fixed signs are Taurus, Leo, Scorpio and Aquarius. The mutable signs are Gemini, Virgo, Sagittarius and Pisces. A value of one point is given for each sign tenanted by a planet, for a total of ten points. However, for better results one may wish to utilize the following point system which places more emphasis on personal points in the chart. This system will be utilized throughout the book.

Sun, Moon, Ascendant = 4 points each
Mercury, Venus, Mars = 3 points each
Jupiter, Saturn, North Node = 2 points each
Uranus, Neptune, Pluto = 1 point each
Ruler of the Ascendant = 2 points.

The ruler of the Ascendant will be a planet that will be included in the list twice—in planetary value and for being the ruler of the Ascendant.

Using Chart G, which is interpreted in Chapter Four, Assessing Severity and Duration of Disease, with the Sun in Aquarius, the Moon in Leo, Mercury in Pisces, Venus in Aquarius, Mars in Sagittarius, Jupiter in Taurus, Saturn in Taurus, Uranus in Taurus, Neptune in Virgo, Pluto in Leo, the North Node in Libra and the Ascendant in Capricorn, we find:

Cardinal = 4 (Ascendant), 2 (North Node)

Fixed = 4 (Sun), 4 (Moon), 3 (Venus), 2 (Jupiter), 2 (Saturn), 1 (Uranus), 1 (Pluto), 2 (Saturn, as ruler of the Ascendant)

Mutable = 3 (Mercury). 3 (Mars), 1 (Neptune)

The strong emphasis in fixed signs (19 points) may indicate the individual is prone to fixed types of diseases. There are 32 points in all in this system. Look for a majority of points in one quadruplicity as indicating the possibility of propensity to disease in that quadruplicity. Then incorporate the information derived from the point system with the basic steps in giving a health reading. In the above example, it would be appropriate to investigate more fully the possibility of the client manifesting diseases of the fixed quadruplicity.

For greater accuracy and confirmation to determine cardinal, fixed or mutable types of illnesses in the natal chart, check for afflictions in a particular quadruplicity. In *Essentials of Medical Astrology*, Harry F. Darling, M.D. states that "malefics which afflict angles or afflict other planets conjunct angles indicate the greatest susceptibility to illness in the quadruplicity concerned."[8] Thus, afflictions in succedent and cadent houses are not as threatening as afflictions involving the angles. Afflictions to the ruler of a sign can indicate a disturbance in that sign or quadruplicity.

Cardinal type illnesses relate to the signs on the cardinal cross—Aries, Libra, Cancer and Capricorn. They can refer to disorders affecting the head, kidneys, stomach, skin and bones. There can be eye problems, breast disease and other ailments connected with the rulership of these signs. Disease tends to be acute in nature.

Fixed cross illnesses, which relate to signs on the fixed cross—Taurus, Scorpio, Leo and Aquarius—can affect the throat, reproductive and eliminative organs, heart and circulation. The fixed quadruplicity can refer to chronic disease that lasts a long time. The mutable cross—Gemini, Sagittarius, Virgo and Pisces—can indicate diseases associated with the lungs, intestines, nervous system, and immune system. There can be metabolic disturbances. Mutable diseases tend to be acute in nature and sometimes indicate a mental origin.

Along with using the Ascendant/Descendant axis and Midheaven/IC axis in determining quadruplicity emphasis, the Vertex and its opposite, the Antivertex, the third axis of the chart, should be utilized. The Vertex is found at the degree of longitude where the plane of the celestial prime vertical intersects the plane of the ecliptic. The late Charles Jayne, an eminent astrologer, developed the Vertex concept with L. Edward Johndro. He recommended its use as an important factor in chart interpretation. To compute the vertex:

1. Find the co-latitude for the chart by subtracting the birth latitude from ninety degrees. For a New York City chart at 40N45, ninety degrees minus

40N45 equals 49N15, the co-latitude.

2. Take the degree opposite the Midheaven which is the same as the IC.

3. In any tables of houses look up this new Midheaven at the co-latitude.

4. The Ascendant at this co-latitude will be the Vertex of the chart. It is found on the western side of the chart generally falling between the fifth and ninth houses.

The Vertex is thought to relate to fate or karma. Interpretation depends on its sign, house position and aspects. It should be considered in analyzing quadruplicity emphasis as planets conjunct the Vertex or Antivertex indicate first degree tendency to illness according to the quadruplicity it tenants.

There is another axiom in astrology that states that planets which are conjunct angles are square to each other whether or not the aspect exists in longitude. The term used is mundane square or *in mundo*. These planets are rising or culminating at the same time. In a medical reading, this could describe planets acting as if in square, thus afflicting their respective angles and afflicting a particular quadruplicity.

Step Five—Examining Midpoints Relating to Health

After examining the quadruplicities, the next step is to examine the health midpoints in the chart. This will give more information as to specific health disorders. First examine the Sun/Moon midpoint. Planets aspecting this midpoint can affect the health and vitality—with Mars and Jupiter increasing it and Saturn and Neptune depleting it. Pluto aspecting the Sun/Moon midpoint can indicate bodily transformation and an aspect from Uranus may indicate a circulatory disorder.

For chronic illness or bodily weakness, examine the Mars/Saturn and the Saturn/Neptune midpoints. A personal point equaling one of these two midpoints could be indicative of a health disorder. In *Astrology, Key to Holistic Health*, Marcia Starck also recommends examining the Mars/Uranus midpoint which she states corresponds "to the nervous system, injuries, accidents or operations," the Mars/Pluto midpoint, which she states refers to "heavy accidents, destruction of cells or destruction of life in some form" and the Mars/Neptune midpoint, "the point of toxicity, susceptibility to infections, epidemics, toxic conditions from poisons and drugs."[9] There is an excellent chapter in her book describing these health midpoints and their interpretation as well as information on three planets found in a T-square or a midpoint combination. Again, it is the involvement of a personal point with these midpoint combinations that indicates the greatest susceptibility to disease.

Step Six—Analyzing Resistance to Disease

Information on resistance to disease can be determined by analyzing the point count of planets in the elements fire, earth, air and water. Too little emphasis in fire can indicate a lack of the fiery energy needed to resist disease. There can also be a lack of physical vitality and poor digestion. Too much fire can describe a person who burns himself or herself out. This type must learn how to conserve physical energy.

Those with a lack of the earth element tend to have poor health habits, thus ignoring the needs of the body. Those with a preponderance of earth usually take good care of themselves; however, they may become overly obsessed with health. Those with an abundance of air signs tend toward overactive minds that can lead to nervous exhaustion. The nervous system is highly activated and extremely sensitive. These people need periods of rest and relaxation to allow the nervous system to recharge itself. A lack of air can indicate a difficulty in the flow of bodily energies and may indicate a weak nervous system.

An abundance of water in the chart can be descriptive of a person with emotional problems or one who is overly sensitive to environmental influences. It can also indicate excess fluid in the tissues of the body. The water abundance, however is an aid in eliminating toxins from the body. A lack of the water element can indicate a difficulty in eliminating toxins from the body. This type should drink plenty of water every day and periodically engage in diets that cleanse the body.

In general, the ability to fight disease is enhanced by a fire and air emphasis, an angular Mars or Jupiter, a well placed Sun, and a Pluto or Scorpio emphasis. Mutable planets also have the ability to throw off disease. Heindel gives Aries, Gemini, Leo, Libra and Aquarius as having the ability to overcome and fight disease and Taurus and Virgo as the weakest, due to lack of will power to rise above physical conditions.[10] Along with resistance to disease is one's ability to eliminate toxins from the body. Rulerships of planets and signs dealing with the processes of elimination—the bowels, kidneys, lungs, skin and the mucous membranes—should be examined. Retention of toxins is considered by many health practitioners to be a major cause of disease.

Determining the speed and slowness of the metabolism is an aid in judging resistance to disease. The process of metabolism is a complex one involving the endocrine system, absorption of food and utilization of oxygen. Davidson described the metabolism as the ''fire of life'' and felt that despite difficult physical problems, a good metabolism can burn up toxins in the body.[11] Afflictions to the Sun from Mars, Saturn, Uranus, Neptune or Pluto can alter the metabolism. Generally, Mars and Pluto increase the metabolism, Saturn slows it down, Uranus causes an erratic metabolism and Neptune weakens it. In *Mind and Body in Astrology*, Ronald Harvey found fire and then air signs and a prominent Sun, Mars and Jupiter to indicate a high metabolism. He finds Taurus and Capricorn and then water signs with Moon, Venus and Saturn prominent to indicate a lowered metabolism. He finds that cardinal and mutable signs increase the metabolic rate and fixed signs decrease it.[12]

Supporting metabolic activity is one's oxidation level. Saturn in Aquarius or Saturn in hard aspect to a Sun, Moon or Ascendant in Aquarius can indicate poor oxidation. Mars in Aquarius or Mars in good aspect to the Sun, Moon or Ascendant in Aquarius indicates high oxidation. Good adrenal action, as shown by a prominent and well aspected Mars (ruler of adrenal action) can counteract signatures indicating poor oxidation.

Chart A—Example

Chart A illustrates the use of steps one through six in analyzing a natal chart. The chart is that of a female who wished to know what her chart showed in

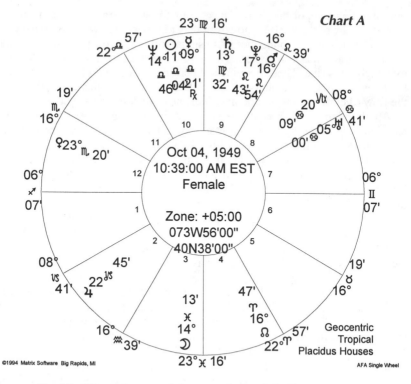

Chart A

23°♍16'

22°♎57'

Ψ ☉ ☿
14°11°09°
♎ ♎ ♎
46'04'21'
℞

ℏ 13° ♍ 32'

Ψ ♂
17° 16°
16°
♌ ♌
43' 54'

16°♌39'

19'
♏
16°

20°♐08°
09'♋ ♋
00'♋ 05°♅ 41'

♀23°♏20'

10

9

8

06°
♐
07'

12

Oct 04, 1949
10:39:00 AM EST
Female

Zone: +05:00
073W56'00"
40N38'00"

7

6

06°
♊
07'

11

1

2

5

3   4

08°
♑
41'

45'

22°♑

4

13'
♓
14°
☽

47'
♈
16°
♌
22°♈57'

19'
♉
16°

16°
♒39'

23°♓16'

Geocentric
Tropical
Placidus Houses

©1994 Matrix Software Big Rapids, MI

AFA Single Wheel

terms of health. Her major complaints were lack of vitality, headaches, insomnia, dysmenorrhea, and a difficulty in losing weight. She had also been diagnosed as having a disease of a valve in the heart with a consequent heart murmur.

Sun

Her Sun is afflicted in Libra in the tenth house. The Sun is quincunx the Moon. A hard aspect between the Sun and the Moon can indicate lowered vitality and a disturbance in health. The quincunx is considered to be an aspect affecting health and work. There is a need for compromise, readjustment or reassessment according to the planets and houses involved. The Sun-Moon quincunx can indicate a conflict between the emotions and the conscious will that needs to be adjusted. In *Planets in Aspect*, Robert Pelletier states that persons with this aspect abuse their health by yielding to the demands others make on their time and energy. Somehow, these people feel they owe it to others. A person with this configuration must learn to relax and get away as often as possible to unwind from daily pressures.[13] A tenth house Sun can describe a person driven toward success, and in this case with the quincunx to the Moon in the third house, this could describe day-to-day pressures resulting in the client's usual feeling of exhaustion. And with Mercury's rulership of the nervous system, the client's conjunction of Mercury to the Sun could contribute to nervous exhaustion and tension headaches. The client's Sun square Uranus

18

indicates an erratic energy level exacerbated by Mercury's square to Uranus—another example of nervous exhaustion and frayed nerves. Certainly the square of Mercury to Uranus could contribute to difficulty in sleeping as the client may be unable to shut off her mind to relax enough to get a good night's sleep.

The client's Sun is semisextile Saturn. As mentioned, the semisextile is like a quincunx in that inharmonious signs are brought into play. Although this is a minor aspect, it contributes to the overall picture of a person with an energy problem. Saturn can indicate limits to the vitality, possibly due to overwork, and with her tenth house Sun, there may be a self-imposed pressure to prove herself to the world. Sun is conjunct Neptune, an aspect descriptive of depletion of vitality and bodily weakness. With a hard aspect between the Sun and Neptune a person may take longer to heal, be subject to infection due to a weakened immune system, and have difficulty in being diagnosed. With Neptune's conjunction to the Sun, it is possible for a client to be misinformed or misdiagnosed regarding health problems. A prominent Neptune or Neptune in hard aspect to a personal point can indicate a drug sensitive individual. This type usually requires only half the usual dosage of medication prescribed by a doctor. The client's Sun is parallel Neptune, reinforcing the natal Sun conjunct Neptune.

Her Sun 11 Libra 04 – Mercury/Neptune 12 Aries/Libra 04. This midpoint configuration can indicate weak nerves and sensitivity. However, her Sun = Pluto/Ascendant 11 Aries/55. This would add to her physical vitality and allow the opportunity for bodily transformation leading to better health.

Moon

The chart contains a Pisces Moon involved in a yod formation with Mars conjunct Pluto and a conjunction of Sun, Mercury, and Neptune. The closest aspect in the yod is the exact quincunx of Neptune to the Moon. The involvement of so many planets with two personal points could result in health complications. The close opposition of Saturn to the Moon further alters the client's health. With the Moon the focal point of the yod, her physical problems could have an emotional basis. Repression (Moon opposite Saturn) can alternate with excessive emotionality (Moon in Pisces, Moon quincunx Neptune, Moon quincunx Mars conjunct Pluto) resulting in a lack of emotional balance or emotional confusion that is expressed as physical illness. Certainly, the client's emotional state is highly complex and inconsistent due to the influence of the yod. Since the natal Moon deals with emotional needs, denial or repression could manifest as physical illness. The afflictions to the Moon could indicate disturbances to the menstrual cycle. And with the Moon's rulership of fluids and mucous production, her afflicted Moon could indicate water retention or mucous production leading to sluggishness and fatigue. Note also the client's Moon contraparallel Saturn—a reinforcement of the Moon opposite Saturn.

The client's interest in occult and creative pursuits is a positive use of the vague Piscean energy of the Moon and offers a way to overcome her confusion, uncertainty and extremist tendencies toward a more consistent form of self-assertion (Moon quincunx Mars) and self-initiative.

Ascendant

An analysis of the Ascendant shows a Sagittarius Ascendant receiving a sextile from the conjunction of Sun and Mercury. Sagittarius, being a fire sign, is a good conductor of energy but it should be noted that due to its mutable nature, the energy flow may not always be constant. The quincunx of Uranus to the Ascendant also indicates an erratic flow of energy. It is also descriptive of a "hyper" personality type who needs to learn how to relax. The Sagittarius Ascendant could also play a part in the client's weight problem, especially since the ruler, Jupiter, is semisquare the Ascendant and posited in the natural house of Taurus—all related to food and excess. Jupiter is also contraparallel the Ascendant—reinforcing the semisquare. But in all, it is the optimism and hopeful outlook of a Sagittarius rising that can help client overcome her health problems.

Quadruplicity Emphasis

There can be health ailments relating to the fixed quadruplicity since the Mars Pluto conjunction in Leo is square Venus in Scorpio. The client has stated she has a heart murmur. With Pluto being a higher vibration of Mars and with the fixed nature of Leo, her heart may be overworking itself. Heart action is also weakened by Neptune's conjunction to the Sun which afflicts the sign Leo. Mars conjunct Pluto square Venus in Scorpio can also be an indication of a functional disorder with the female menstrual cycle.

Using the point system discussed earlier, the client's chart contains a majority of planets in cardinal signs—twelve points. This cardinal emphasis is also strengthened by three planets and the South Node in the tenth house—a cardinal house. There are ten points in mutability, so the medical astrologer should examine this axis also, especially since the Ascendant, Midheaven and the Moon are all in mutable signs.

There are no close conjunctions to angles. Natal Moon is nine degrees from the IC and natal Saturn is ten degrees from the MC. This may be too wide an orb to be considered as a conjunction. Yet Saturn's position as the most elevated planet in the chart in close opposition to the Moon makes this an affliction in mutable signs and also adds weight to the emphasis in cardinal signs, as Saturn afflicts the Moon—ruler of the sign Cancer. Though not conjunct an angle, the Sun is in an angular house and afflicted by Neptune, which also afflicts Mercury—all cardinal. To add further emphasis to this cardinal emphasis note also Jupiter's conjunction to the Antivertex—adding to the cardinal emphasis of the chart. And due to the nature of Jupiter, any difficulties can be expanded.

The client has health problems relating to all three quadruplicities; however, the greatest emphasis is in the cardinal quadruplicity.

Midpoints

An examination of the health midpoints finds the Moon 14 Pisces 13 = Mars/Neptune 15 Virgo/Pisces 50. With the Moon ruling Cancer, this could indicate infection or toxicity in any of the areas ruled by Cancer. She may be prone to nausea, vomiting, stomach upsets caused by bacteria and food poisoning. She may suffer allergic reactions to certain foods, possibly milk

20

products.

The client's Neptune at 14 Libra 46 is semisquare/sesquiquadrate Mars/Saturn at 00 Virgo/Pisces 13. This midpoint configuration does not involve any personal points and is a minor aspect. With Neptune's rulership of Pisces, this would be more corroboration of a lowered immune system (Sun conjunct Neptune) and lowered vitality. Of itself, it would be only a minor problem.

Resistance To Disease

In the client's chart, the four major angles are all in mutable signs, giving her the ability to throw off disease. Since mutable signs are associated with the mind, a study of health and nutrition could aid client in understanding her own health problems. Mutability also implies dispersiveness—she need not hold onto these problems. And the mutable emphasis also implies that by the use of meditation and positive thinking, she may alleviate some of her problems.

The client's Mars-Pluto conjunction in fire indicates acute reaction to disease. Despite the fact that she is prone to infections and fevers, this is an indication of her body fighting toxic conditions—the fever burns off the toxins. A difficult aspect between the Sun and Saturn or an angular Saturn can indicate a person who may suffer from a chronic disease, have difficulty burning up toxins or difficulty in fighting disease. Although the client has the ability to fight disease, there will be times when this ability is impeded or slowed down. This can be seen by the elevated status of Saturn semisextile the Sun and opposite the Moon. This, plus Neptune afflicting the Sun, indicates a need for rest and relaxation in order to avoid the colds and flus associated with this combination. A proper diet is essential to aid her immune system. It should also be noted that the times the client is ill depends on the transits, progressions and directions in operation at the time.

The client has a wide sextile of the Sun to Mars which tends to increase the metabolism. However, with Sun square Uranus, metabolic activity will be erratic. The close aspect of Neptune to the Sun weakens the metabolism. Her fire sign rising and predominance of cardinal planets increases the metabolism. But her afflicted Moon in water opposite Saturn and the focal point of the yod probably decreases the metabolism. In all, the client would benefit from physical exercise and breathing exercises to overcome the lack of tone resulting from Neptune's conjunction to the Sun.

There are no obvious indications of poor oxidation in chart. And the Sun-Mars sextile aids adrenal action.

Step Seven—Determining Specific Disease States

While analyzing the chart for general health conditions, certain attributes relating to health will be repeated in much the same way as character traits are repeated or shown through different signatures in the natal chart. The more indications one finds of a particular disorder, the more likely it is to be a possible health concern for the client. In a natal chart reading one may list various traits under categories such as mentality, vocation, etc. This same idea can be used in a medical reading. The medical astrologer can list specific categories according to client's complaints, list categories of particular problems that are repeated in the chart and/or check for traits associated with various astrological signatures for disease.

The following categories of health disorders can be used as a guide to assess probability and severity of a health disorder as seen in the natal chart. The list is by no means inclusive or limiting. There are many variables, such as heredity, health habits, age, and sex that must be considered along with the natal chart. But, as stated above, as one notes a repetition of astrological significators occurring in the various categories, one will get a better idea of a client's propensity to a particular disorder. The reader is also referred to the following medical astrology books which list specific astrological indications of disease:

1. *An Encyclopaedia of Psychological Astrology* by C.E.O. Carter
2. *Astro-Diagnosis A Guide to Healing* by Max Heindel
3. *Astrology Key to Holistic Health* by Marcia Starck
4. *Astrology: 30 Years Research* by Doris Chase Doane
5. *Casenotes of a Medical Astrologer* by Margaret Millard M.D.
6. *Encyclopaedia of Medical Astrology* by H.L. Cornell, M.D.
7. *Medical Astrology* by Heinrich Daath
8. *Mind and Body in Astrology* by Ronald Harvey
9. *Modern Medical Astrology* by Robert C. Jansky

These categories should be read as possible indicators of an illness or health disorder. Keep in mind the earlier steps which delineate propensity and resistance to disease and look for several repetitions on a theme before making definitive statements. The last section of this book will give information on how to determine severity and duration of disease.

Propensity to Auto-Immune Diseases (Lowered Immune System)

- Sun or Moon afflicted by Saturn or Neptune.
- Preponderance of mutability.
- Twelfth house emphasis; afflicted Sun in twelfth house.
- Neptune angular or prominent.
- Jupiter involved in a T-square or grand cross.
- Afflictions involving Mars, ruler of adrenal activity.
- Saturn in Pisces or Virgo or in the twelfth house.
- Mars square Neptune, Mars in Pisces.
- Afflictions to planets in Pisces.
- Neptune heavily afflicted.

Harvey gives rulership of the lymphatic system to the Moon, Neptune, Cancer, the fourth house and its ruler.[14] Cornell gives the lymph system to the Moon, Aquarius and Pisces and water signs in general.[15]

Midpoint combinations thought to be involved include:

- Sun = Mars/Saturn
- Sun = Saturn/Neptune
- Sun = Mars/Neptune
- Neptune = Sun/Mars
- Neptune = Sun/Saturn
- Neptune = Sun/Moon

- Mars = Saturn/Neptune
- Midheaven = Mars/Neptune

Nervous Disorders
- Gemini or Virgo emphasis.
- Mercury angular and afflicted.
- Preponderance of mutability.
- Mutable T-square or grand cross.
- Afflictions to planet or planets in Gemini or to Mercury.
- Third or sixth house emphasis.
- Mercury afflicted by Mars or Uranus.
- Preponderance of air signs.
- Uranus angular.
- Sun in Gemini, Sagittarius or Aquarius afflicted.
- Saturn or Neptune in a mutable sign.
- Afflictions to ruler of third or ninth house.
- Malefics in third house or conjunct third house cusp.
- Mercury in Aries afflicted.
- Mercury afflicting Sun or Moon.
- Mars Uranus in hard aspect.
- Uranus in hard aspect to Ascendant.
- Mercury opposite Neptune (weak nerves).

Midpoint configurations include:
- Sun = Mars/Uranus
- Sun = Uranus/Pluto
- Mercury = Mars/Pluto
- Mercury = Saturn/Uranus
- Mercury = Saturn/Neptune
- Mercury = Mars/Uranus
- Uranus = Mercury/Pluto
- Uranus = Sun/Neptune
- Uranus = Mercury/Saturn
- Pluto = Mercury/Uranus

Weight Problem
- Angular Jupiter afflicted by outer planet or planets.
- Jupiter in sixth house.
- Jupiter in water sign.
- Cancer, Taurus, or Sagittarius rising—ruler afflicted.
- Emphasis in Cancer or Pisces.
- Sun or Moon in Cancer or Taurus.
- Second house emphasis.
- Venus in hard aspect to Jupiter.
- Stellium in Taurus.

- Moon-Jupiter conjunction or opposition.
- Venus in Taurus or Cancer in aspect to Mars.

Carter gives Jupiter usually afflicted by Saturn or Uranus usually in Gemini, Virgo or Capricorn; fixed signs except Scorpio and Sun or Moon in Aquarius; Cancer and Pisces [16]

Allergies

There are different kinds of allergies. Common to most is a prominent Neptune or Moon or a combination of both; Neptune in the sixth house may also contribute to allergies.

Respiratory allergies:
- Preponderance of mutable signs.
- Mercury prominent.
- Saturn in the third house.
- Afflictions involving Mercury, Gemini, Sagittarius, or Virgo.
- Mercury-Saturn in hard aspect.

Asthma is a respiratory allergy with the following signature:
- Saturn afflictions to the third house; Saturn in the third house.
- Afflictions in Gemini.
- Mutable afflictions/preponderance of mutability.
- Mercury prominent.
- Saturn in Gemini or Sagittarius.
- Neptune afflicting Sun or Moon.
- Gemini or Sagittarius emphasis.
- Mercury-Saturn affliction.
- Angular Moon, emphasis in Cancer.
- Moon in Virgo or Sagittarius.
- Taurus or Scorpio prominent.
- Uranus in Gemini.

Carter gives tenancy of eighteen degrees Gemini/Sagittarius and four degrees Virgo/Pisces. [17] There will be other factors involved depending on the cause of the asthma.

Hay fever is a respiratory allergy with the following signature:
- Mutable preponderance.
- Prominent Mercury.
- Sagittarius or Gemini emphasis.
- Mercury-Saturn in hard aspect.
- Prominent Neptune.
- Sun in Gemini.
- Afflictions in Taurus/Scorpio.

Carter found Aries and signs of Saturn prominent and the Moon in either Capricorn or Aquarius. [18]

Skin allergies:
- Venus-Saturn in hard aspect.

- Saturn in Cancer or Capricorn.
- Capricorn rising.
- Mars in Capricorn.
- Venus-Mars or Venus-Pluto afflictions.
- Afflictions in Aries/Libra.
- Aries can refer to burns and blisters and Libra to dermatitis; Moon—swellings; Mars—rashes; Pluto—skin growths.

Eczema, a skin allergy with the following signature:
- Afflictions in Capricorn.
- Prominent Mars or Pluto.
- Mars in Aries or Libra.
- Venus afflicted.
- Afflictions to Libra or Aries.
- Saturn or Capricorn afflicted.

Carter gives twenty-eight degrees Virgo/Pisces, Mars and Neptune in affliction and difficulties with Venus and Libra. Also fifteen degrees Libra and possibly Saturn affliction to the Ascendant.[19]

Hives, a skin allergy with the following signature:
- Mars prominent
- Venus afflictions to outer planets.
- Mars afflictions in Capricorn.
- Capricorn rising.
- Prominent or afflicted Moon.
- Saturn in mutable sign.
- Mercury-Saturn affliction.
- Moon-Mars in hard aspect.

Stomach allergies:
- Emphasis in cardinal signs.
- Moon in the sixth house.
- Cancer rising—afflicted.
- Moon-Mars in hard aspect.
- Venus-Jupiter in hard aspect.
- Prominent Moon or emphasis in Cancer.
- Cancer on the cusp of the sixth house.
- Hard aspects to Moon.

Kidney Disorder

- Saturn, Uranus, or Neptune in Libra or Aries and receiving hard aspects.
- Hard aspects to Sun in Libra or Aries.
- Venus in Aries/Libra afflicted.
- Venus-Saturn in hard aspect.
- Stellium in the seventh house.
- Afflictions in Libra or Aries.

- Afflictions in cardinal signs.
- Venus afflicted.
- Mars in Libra or Aries.
- Afflictions to ruler of the seventh house.
- Saturn in the seventh house.
- Saturn in Aries or Libra.

Doane's analysis of 100 charts for kidney trouble found ninety-nine percent with Venus afflicted, ninety-seven percent with Mars afflicted and ninety-six percent with Pluto afflicted.[20] Pluto rulership may refer to the pelvic area of kidneys.

Stomach and Intestinal Disorders

Stomach disorders can manifest as:
- Afflictions in Cancer or Capricorn.
- Afflictions to the Moon.
- Cancer on the sixth house cusp.
- Fourth house emphasis.
- Mars or Saturn in Cancer.
- Emphasis in cardinal signs.
- Moon afflicted by Jupiter, Mars, or Uranus.
- Cancer/Capricorn emphasis.
- Ruler of the fourth house afflicted.
- Uranus in Cancer.
- Mars or Saturn in hard aspect to Sun, Moon or Ascendant and involvement of sign Cancer.
- Mercury involved when digestive disturbances caused by nerves.
- Mars-Neptune involved in food poisoning.

Intestinal disorders may manifest as:
- Mars or Saturn in Virgo or Pisces.
- Afflictions to the Sun or Moon in Virgo or Pisces.
- Mercury afflicted and planet in Virgo or Pisces involved.
- Mutable emphasis.
- Virgo rising.
- Virgo on the cusp of the sixth house.
- Jupiter afflicted in Virgo.
- Virgo/Pisces prominent and afflicted.

Colon or large intestine disorders may manifest as:
- Scorpio emphasis.
- Sun or Moon in the eighth house.
- Eighth house emphasis.
- Mars-Pluto afflictions.
- Mars-Uranus afflictions (spastic colon).
- Scorpio rising.
- Fixed emphasis.

- Mars or Saturn in Scorpio.
- Pluto prominent.
- Mercury-Mars—bowel irritation.
- Mercury-Saturn or Mars-Saturn—constipation.
- Sun, Moon Ascendant in Scorpio and afflicted or receiving hard aspects from planets in Scorpio.
- Virgo or Mercury involvement—bowel trouble caused by nerves; also Uranus involved.
- Uranus in Scorpio or Taurus.

Blood Sugar Disorder

Diabetes and hypoglycemia are diseases of metabolism related to the pancreas. There is no real agreement among medical astrologers on this signature. The following are possibilities:

- Afflictions to Venus.
- Second house emphasis.
- Saturn in Virgo.
- Jupiter affliction.
- Emphasis in fixed signs.
- Mars or Pluto afflicting another planet.
- Prominent Neptune.
- Mars or Saturn in Virgo.
- Afflictions in Taurus.
- Jupiter or Venus in Libra afflicted.
- Stellium in Taurus.

Carter gives seventeen degrees Cancer/Capricorn, planets in Aries and Libra, Sun Uranus afflictions, Jupiter Uranus afflictions, Mars, Saturn and Neptune in aspect or two of them, Mercury Mars afflictions.[21] Doane found Saturn and Jupiter afflicted and frequently with each other.[22]

Gynecolological Disorders

There is no real agreement as to rulership of the ovaries—either Scorpio and a fixed emphasis or Cancer and Venus and a cardinal emphasis. The following are possible signatures for gynecological disorders:

- Venus-Mars in hard aspect.
- Venus or Mars in Scorpio afflicted.
- Moon square Mars.
- Venus in Scorpio afflicting the Moon or Ascendant.
- Moon-Venus influence.
- Sun or Moon afflicted in Scorpio.
- Afflictions in Scorpio.
- Mars-Venus-Pluto in hard aspect.
- Mars-Uranus afflicting Venus.
- Moon afflicted by Sun, Mars, Saturn or Pluto.
- Venus in Scorpio afflicted in the sixth house.

- Venus-Saturn in hard aspect.
- Venus-Neptune in hard aspect.
- Afflictions in Cancer/Capricorn axis.

Possible midpoint configurations include:
- Venus = Mars/Pluto
- Neptune = Moon/Mars
- Saturn = Moon/Venus
- Pluto = Moon/Mars
- Moon = Saturn/Neptune
- Moon = Mars/Neptune
- Pluto = Moon/Venus
- Mars = Venus/Neptune

Respiratory Disorders

- Afflictions in Gemini or Sagittarius.
- Third house emphasis.
- Mercury-Saturn in hard aspect.
- Ruler of third house afflicted.
- Mercury prominent.
- Saturn in Gemini or Sagittarius.
- Mutable emphasis.
- Saturn in third house.
- Moon-Saturn in hard aspect.
- Mars-Saturn-Neptune in hard aspect.
- Mercury = Mars/Saturn

Blood Disorders

- Mars-Neptune or Mars-Neptune-Pluto indicates blood poisoning or toxemia.
- Afflictions to Jupiter, ruler of arterial blood circulation.
- Afflictions to Venus, ruler of venous blood circulation.
- Mars rules iron level in blood, Saturn is involved in blood clots and oxygenation of blood involves Gemini and Aquarius.

Harmon gives twenty-five degrees Leo/Aquarius for toxic disorder in the blood, especially if Venus is afflicted by Mars or Saturn. She gives twenty-one degrees Aries also.[23]

For anemia Carter gives Sun afflicted by Uranus or in Libra or Aquarius and eight degrees Leo/Aquarius.[24] Harmon gives eight degrees Leo/Aquarius for pernicious anemia.[25]

Doane found Neptune and Saturn prominent and usually afflicted and found Mars also afflicted in cases of blood disorders.[26]

Circulatory Disorders

- Afflictions involving the Sun
- Afflictions to Leo/Aquarius axis or fifth and eleventh houses.
- Saturn in Aquarius.

- Uranus afflicted.
- Venus-Uranus in hard aspect.
- Venus-Saturn-Jupiter in hard aspect.
- Venus-Jupiter or Venus-Neptune in hard aspect.
- Afflictions to Jupiter or Sagittarius or Pisces.
- Emphasis in fixed signs.
- Lack of air.

Varicose veins, a circulatory disorder:
- Afflictions in Aquarius.
- Venus in Aquarius in hard aspect to Saturn.
- Venus-Jupiter in hard aspect.
- Venus-Mars in hard aspect.
- Venus in Aries.
- Prominent Venus and Saturn.

Migraine Disorders
- Signature involving Cancer, Aries, Moon and Mars.
- Saturn in Aries or Libra.
- Moon-Uranus in hard aspect.
- Mercury-Uranus in hard aspect.
- Involvement of Sun, Saturn and Uranus.
- Uranus or Neptune in Aries or Libra and receiving hard aspects.

Endocrine Gland Disorders
Astrologically, this area requires more research using the charts of persons exhibiting glandular disorders. Since there is no agreement among medical astrologers on the rulership of the endocrine glands, it is difficult to list astrological significators of endocrine gland disorders. The hormones secreted by the endocrine glands control and regulate most bodily activity. Referring to the earlier discussion of rulership, it would make sense to give the anatomical location of a gland sign rulership and the physiological action of the hormone to a planet. Due to the complexity and diversity of the individual hormones, they are probably ruled by combinations of planets.

The following is a description of the astrological significators of the endocrine glands. The ruler cited the most frequently in the medical astrology literature will be listed first:

Pituitary gland: Aries, Uranus
Posterior pituitary gland: Cancer, Sagittarius, Jupiter
Anterior pituitary gland: Capricorn, Saturn, Scorpio
Thyroid gland: Taurus, Scorpio, Mercury
Parathyroid gland: Aquarius, Saturn, Venus
Pineal gland: Pisces, Taurus, Neptune
Adrenal glands: Aries, Libra, Mars
Thymus gland: Taurus, Neptune, Gemini, Venus
Pancreas: Virgo
Gonads, ovaries: Scorpio, Cancer, Moon, Venus, Pluto

Testes: Scorpio, Pluto, Sun

Cardiovascular Disorders

- Afflictions to the Sun or to Leo.
- Afflictions to the fifth house cusp or ruler of the fifth house.
- Saturn in Leo.
- Saturn in the fifth house.
- Malefics in the fifth or eleventh houses.
- Saturn in Leo or Aquarius.
- Mars in Leo or Aquarius.
- Afflictions to planets in Aquarius.
- Jupiter-Saturn or Jupiter-Uranus in hard aspect.
- Mars-Uranus afflictions.
- Saturn-Uranus afflictions.
- Sun-Mars-Uranus in hard aspect.
- Leo rising afflicted.
- Uranus angular and fixed aspecting Sun or Moon—rigidity and faulty elimination causing toxins in blood.
- Afflictions in Cancer or cardinal signs—affecting lining of heart
- Jupiter in Capricorn

Step Eight—A Nutritional Assessment of the Chart

Assessing a person's nutritional requirements from the natal chart is easier said than done. This is another area of astrology where one finds little agreement as to the rulership of the various vitamins and minerals. It is certainly an area requiring further research and study, especially since recent scientific evidence has shown there may be a relationship between diet and certain disease states. A perusal of many health magazines will show instances of persons being cured of various health problems by improved nutrition and vitamin and mineral supplementation. If rulership of vitamins and minerals could be determined, the natal chart could be a valuable tool in assessing nutritional deficiencies.

The medical astrology books that give rulership to vitamins and minerals list one planet for the specific vitamin or mineral—for example stating the Sun rules Vitamin A. And among the singular rulerships, there is no agreement. In my opinion, since nothing in nature works alone and since the vitamins and minerals have multiple purposes, it makes more sense for combinations of planets to rule a specific vitamin or mineral. Hence, afflictions and/or a conjunction between these planets may indicate a deficiency state. And in the case where one planet does rule a specific vitamin or mineral—such as Mars ruling the mineral iron—not all afflictions to Mars are indicative of a deficiency. More likely a hard aspect from Neptune to Mars or Saturn to Mars or Mars in Pisces indicates an iron deficiency. A medical astrologer who is versed in nutrition should be able to make an educated guess as to particular nutritional deficiencies as shown in the natal chart. The following is the author's list of rulerships of vitamins and minerals. Some agree with the findings of other medical astrologers; others on the list do not. The list includes the main functions and most common deficiency states associated with each vitamin or mineral listed.

Vitamin A

Ruled by the Sun and/or the following planetary combinations:

- Aids immune system, fatigue, allergies: Sun-Neptune, Sun-Moon, Mars-Neptune.
- Needed for skin: Sun-Venus, Sun-Saturn, Saturn in Capricorn, Venus-Saturn.
- Aids respiratory system: Sun-Mercury, Mercury-Saturn.
- Improves vision and retards night blindness: Sun-Venus, Sun-Mars, Sun-Moon, Sun-Neptune.
- Kidney and bladder function: Sun-Venus, Sun-Pluto, Saturn in Aries or Libra.
- Mucous membranes: Sun-Moon.
- Difficulties in absorption (Vitamin A is fat soluble and requires bile): Sun-Jupiter, Sun-Saturn, Sun-Neptune, Jupiter-Saturn

Vitamin B1—Thiamine

Ruled by Mercury and/or the following planetary combinations:

- Aids nervous system: Mercury, Sun-Mercury, Mercury-Uranus.
- Deficiency causing irritability, insomnia, inability to concentrate: Mercury-Mars, Mercury-Uranus.
- Metabolizes carbohydrates to produce energy: Mercury-Venus, Mercury-Mars.
- Relieves fatigue, firms muscle tone: Mercury-Mars, Mercury-Neptune.

Vitamin B2—Riboflavin

Ruled by Mars and/or the following planetary combinations:

- Aids body in iron absorption from digestive tract: Mars-Moon.
- Needed for proper vision: Mars-Venus, Mars-Moon, Mars-Uranus.
- Energy production: Mars.
- Regulates oxidation: Mars-Uranus, Mars-Saturn, Mars-Mercury, Mars-Sun, Saturn in Aquarius.

Vitamin B3—Niacin

- Aids blood vessels: Venus-Jupiter.
- Aids circulation: Sun-Uranus, Venus-Uranus.
- Protects against stress: Mercury-Mars, Mercury-Uranus, Mercury-Pluto.
- Can aid mental health: Mercury.
- Reduces cholesterol accumulations in the arteries: Jupiter-Saturn.
- Helps cells use oxygen and produces energy: Sun.
- Can counteract blood clotting: Jupiter-Saturn, Venus-Saturn.

Vitamin B5—Pantothenic Acid or Calcium Pantothenate

Ruled by Mars and Neptune and/or the following planetary combinations:

Vitamin K
Necessary for proper human blood coagulation: Mars-Saturn.
Needed for healthy bones: Sun-Saturn.
Can prevent internal bleeding and hemorrhages: Mars, Sun-Jupiter.

Vitamin P—Bioflavonoids
- Builds resistance to infection: Sun-Neptune, Mars-Neptune, Sun-Saturn.
- Presents easy bruising: Saturn.
- Aids circulatory system: Uranus.
- Strengthens capillary walls: Mercury-Saturn.
- Helps prevent bleeding gums: Venus-Saturn.

Calcium
- Necessary for teeth and bones: Saturn.
- Needed for healthy nerves: Mercury.
- Needed for proper blood clotting: Mars-Saturn.
- Helps maintain muscle tone: Mars.
- Needed for healthy heart: Sun.
- Aids iron metabolism: Mars.
- Poor absorption: Jupiter-Saturn, Mars in Capricorn, Saturn-Neptune.

Chromium
- Required for carbohydrate metabolism: Venus.
- Can prevent arterial damage: Jupiter-Saturn.
- Enhances efficiency of insulin: Venus.

Cobalt
- Necessary for synthesis of Vitamin B12: Mars.
- Deficiency causes a progressive nervous disorder: Mercury-Mars.

Copper
- Needed for formation of hemoglobin: Mars.
- Helps prevent cardiovascular disease: Sun-Mars.
- Needed for iron metabolism: Mars.
- Plays a role in many enzyme systems: Pluto.

Iodine
- Essential for proper thyroid activity: Venus-Mars, Venus-Saturn, Saturn in Taurus.
- Promotes healthy hair, nails, skin and teeth: Saturn.

Iron
- Ruled by Mars and/or the following planetary combinations:
- Manufactures hemoglobin in body: Mars, Mars-Neptune, Mars in Pisces.
- Inhibits cholesterol formation in the liver: Jupiter-Saturn.
- Aids growth: Sun.
- Prevents fatigue: Sun-Neptune, Sun-Saturn, Mars-Neptune, Mars-Saturn.

Magnesium
- Necessary for bones and teeth: Saturn.
- Activates many enzymes in the body: Pluto.
- Needed for health of nervous system: Mercury.
- Involved in muscle contraction: Mars.
- Helps prevent heart attacks: Sun-Mars, Sun-Uranus.
- Aids indigestion: Moon, Mars in Cancer.
- Guards against spasms: Uranus.

Manganese
- Helps control glucose tolerance: Venus.
- Assists in fat assimilation: Jupiter.
- Essential to health of prostrate gland: Pluto.
- Necessary for normal bone structure: Saturn.
- Participates in the synthesis of fatty acids and cholesterol: Jupiter.
- Needed for proper digestion: Moon, Moon-Mars.
- Needed for nervous system function: Mercury.

Molybdenum
- Ruled by Mars.
- Necessary for mobilization of iron.
- Increases muscle tone: Mars.
- Aids metabolism: Mars-Neptune.

Phosphorus
- Involved in all bodily activities. Sun.
- Provides energy and vigor: Sun.
- Assists in carbohydrate metabolism: Venus.
- Necessary for assimilation of fats by the body: Jupiter.
- Necessary for heart muscle contraction: Sun.
- Needed for healthy bones and teeth: Saturn.

Potassium
Ruled by the Moon and/or the following planetary combinations:
- Needed for proper working of the digestive tract: Moon.
- Maintains correct concentration and amount of fluids in tissues: Moon.
- Needed for proper excretion of water: Moon.
- Needed for muscle function: Mars.
- Needed to preserve proper alkalinity of body fluids: Mars-Saturn.
- Needed for nerve health: Mercury.
- Can reduce blood pressure: Jupiter.
- Transmits contraction signals to the cardiac muscle: Sun-Uranus.

Selenium
- Helps prevent cellular aging: Jupiter-Saturn.
- Detoxifier: Pluto, Sun-Neptune.
- Stimulates the production of antibodies: Sun-Neptune.

Sodium
- Important for maintenance of body fluid volume: Moon.
- Aids in preventing heat prostration or sunstroke: Sun.
- Sodium imbalance: Mars-Neptune.

Sulphur
- Needed for hair, skin and nails: Saturn.
- Helps fight bacterial infections: Sun-Neptune.
- Aids in metabolism: Mars.

Vanadium
- Inhibits the formation of cholesterol in blood vessels: Jupiter-Saturn.

Zinc
- Needed in all metabolic functions: Mars.
- Needed for healing: Sun-Neptune.
- Helps form skin, nails and hair: Saturn.
- Protects against some heavy metals: Mars-Saturn.
- Necessary for sense of taste and smell: Venus-Saturn.
- Needed for reproductive organs: Mars, Pluto.
- Needed for general growth: Sun.

The preceding list of astrological significators for vitamins and minerals can be used as both a guide to medical chart interpretation and as a stimulus to the reader for further study. In order to make a proper nutritional assessment of a chart, one needs not only a background in astrology, but should be well versed in the study of nutrition. In fact, one does not have to have a birth chart to determine nutritional deficiencies as medical practitioners and nutritionists are trained to recognize vitamin and mineral deficiencies. The natal chart is another tool that can be used as an aid to confirmation.

The preceding list gave the most important functions of the vitamins and minerals listed. By using the rulerships given, one may observe a particular deficiency or deficiencies of vitamins and minerals based on the prominence of and afflictions to a single ruler or based on afflictions between co-rulers. Again, the preceding list is more a listing of educated guesses than scientific fact. Its use should be correlated with clients' complaints and health disorders as shown in the natal chart. It should also be mentioned that one should not indiscriminately take vitamins and minerals as some are known to be toxic. One may advise a client of his or her vitamin and mineral deficiencies as shown in the natal chart, but then the client should be referred to the proper medical authority.

Chart B—Example

The following discussion will provide examples of the use of the list of astrological significators for disease and the list of rulership of vitamins and minerals. Chart B is the chart of a female who suffers from insomnia. She also suffers from severe anxiety for which she is receiving help in psychoanalysis. In examining the natal chart, one can see many significators under "nervous

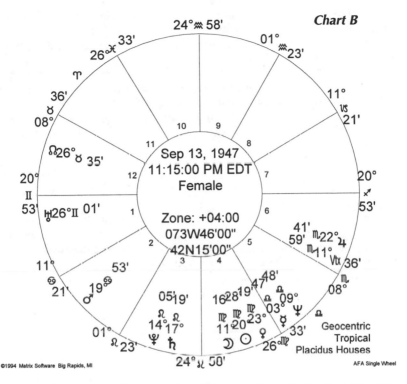

Sep 13, 1947
11:15:00 PM EDT
Female

Zone: +04:00
073W46'00"
42N15'00"

Geocentric
Tropical
Placidus Houses

©1994 Matrix Software Big Rapids, MI

AFA Single Wheel

disorders." There is both a Gemini and Virgo emphasis in the chart. The rising sign is Gemini and there are three planets in Virgo—the Sun, Moon, and Venus. The chart shows a preponderance of mutability with sixteen points. Mercury, ruler of both Gemini and Virgo, is octile Saturn and conjunct Neptune. Uranus in Gemini is conjunct the Ascendant and square the Sun and Venus. There is a preponderance of air signs especially if one considers that the Ascendant and Midheaven are in air. Uranus is angular. The Sun, ruler of the third house is afflicted by a square from Uranus. Malefics in the third can be seen by the tenancy of Saturn and Pluto. One of the deficiencies of thiamine, or B1, in reference to insomnia, is a hard aspect between Mercury Mars or between Mercury and Uranus. Although client does not have either one of these aspects in her chart, she does have Uranus rising in Gemini. Due to its angular nature, her Uranus in Gemini is similar to a hard aspect between Mercury and Uranus. Thus, she should discuss with her physician a possible need for B1. It should be noted that one should not take supplements of an individual B vitamin. The B-complex vitamins should be taken together for an imbalance may lead to deficiency of the other members of the complex. The nervous system is also aided by vitamin B5—pantothenic acid. One of its rulers is Mercury, a planet afflicted in client's chart and the ruler of both her Ascendant and Sun.

Vitamin B6 aids against stress. One of its rulers, Uranus, is rising in the chart and in hard aspect to her Sun. Vitamin B12 aids in maintaining the health

37

of the nervous system. One of its rulers is Mercury. The mineral magnesium is ruled by Mercury in its maintenance of the health of the nervous system. A lack of magnesium may contribute to insomnia. Magnesium is best taken with twice the amount of calcium.

It is beneficial to eat foods containing the vitamins or minerals one is lacking. B-complex is found in such foods as whole grains, nuts, liver, Brewer's yeast, wheat germ, and rice polish. Vitamin B12 occurs only in animal foods. Good sources of magnesium include whole wheat, almonds, cashews, Brazil nuts, pecans, barley, lima beans, beet greens, soy flour and oatmeal.

It would appear that the client would benefit from optimal nutrition from foods containing B-complex and magnesium and should discuss with her physician the advisability of taking supplements of B-Complex, calcium and magnesium.

In giving a health reading, the medical astrologer should utilize the list of astrological significators of diseases and vitamins and minerals and their rulerships in the manner described above. One will be able to correlate planets with deficiencies and be able to see a repetition of either significators for a particular disease state or rulerships of various vitamins and minerals.

Chapter Three

Assessing Severity and Duration of Disease

sing a combination of chart analysis and predictive techniques, the medical astrologer may be able to determine whether or not a medical condition is chronic or acute. The progress of the disease, as well as its severity, can be observed through various predictive methods. However, the exact duration of a disease is not so easily observed.

Using Predictive Techniques in Medical Astrology

Severity of disease is based on the transits, progressions, solar arc directions and eclipses and lunations affecting the natal chart at the time of a particular illness. All information is listed and compared to the natal chart. It is helpful to check back a year or two before the onset of the illness as it may be possible to see cosmic influences that correlate with the present condition. Examine very carefully the day and/or month an illness began.

Charts can also be drawn up for the moment of a diagnosis from a doctor (called the decumbiture chart), the time of surgery, admittance to a hospital, etc. These inception charts can be compared to the natal chart or read separately to furnish extra information. Charts drawn up for the moment of a heart attack or stroke, for example, may furnish information not found through other methods. The inception chart is also useful for analyzing illness when the birth time is unknown.

To determine the severity or duration of an actual illness, predictive techniques for anywhere from one to several years after the onset of a disease can be utilized. For a general health reading, it is unnecessary to utilize predictive techniques; if desired, one year at a time is usually adequate. Normally, predictive techniques are not used to predict illness. Rather, these techniques would be used to advise about times of greater stress, lowered vitality or a tendency to infection.

The same rules for interpreting transits, directions and progressions in natal astrology apply in medical astrology. Transits of the outer planets are more difficult and longer lasting than inner planet transits; aspects from the progressed Sun are quite potent and can last up to two years; solar arc directions can be used as timers in that they move approximately five minutes a month. Aspects involving the ruler of the Ascendant can influence health. One should also observe progressions and directions to the major health midpoints. Severity and duration of disease can be determined by analyzing the combination of influences operative after the onset of the disease. An illness should not be considered serious unless predictions involve a personal point—Sun, Moon, Ascendant or Midheaven. Predictive techniques to the Vertex can also indicate a major health disorder. A major illness will be shown by a combination of planetary influences, usually including an eclipse, and rarely by a single difficult aspect.

Transits

The first step is to list the transits for the period in question. The medical astrologer can get a general idea of a person's health over the course of a year by examining the transiting planets to the natal chart. The forty-five degree graphic ephemeris is a useful tool for seeing the year as a whole. Lines representing the zodiacal positions of the planets, the Ascendant, Midheaven and North Node of the Moon are drawn across the ephemeris. One can also draw lines indicating the positions of the health midpoints. Where the lines drawn intersect with the lines of the transiting planets is the month and day of a particular transit.

Transits of the Sun and the Moon

Transits from the Sun last only a day, applying to and separating from a given point. Increased vitality may be seen when the Sun transits the angles. Resistance may be lowered when the Sun opposes itself.

The transiting Moon moves too quickly to influence health; however, it should be taken into account when one has the opportunity for elective surgery.

Transits of Mercury, Venus and Mars

Mercury and Venus do not have more than a transitory effect on health. However, depending on the aspect, transiting Mercury can indicate tension or anxiety.

Adverse Venus transits can indicate a lack of bodily tone or overindulgence that affects health.

Transiting Mars can act as a trigger or energizer that sets off an outer planet transit. By transit, it can also indicate the onset of fever, inflammation, pain, accident or infection, depending on what it is aspecting.

Transits of Jupiter

Jupiter transits can augment a health condition for better or worse. Jupiter transiting the Sun or Moon can bring increased well-being and emotional fulfillment. Negatively, there can be illness due to excess.

Jupiter to Mercury could aid health by bestowing confidence and optimism. Negatively, there could be a worsening of a lung condition.

Jupiter to Venus is usually a happy occasion. Negatively, there can be self-indulgence in rich foods.

Jupiter to Mars can increase the blood supply; in combination with other afflictions, it could intensify a fever or infection.

Jupiter transiting Saturn could bring healing to a Saturn related illness, clear an obstruction or produce a stress-related ailment caused by tension.

Jupiter to Uranus could bring a sudden healing or a release from pain.

Jupiter to Neptune could put one in a false reality or could indicate a quack cure.

Jupiter to Pluto could improve a blood condition or aid in healing. If it is part of a combination that is badly afflicted, Jupiter to Pluto could be an indication of cell proliferation.

Transits of Saturn

Transits from Saturn can be limiting, constricting, debilitating or can indicate hardening. A Saturn transit can describe a chronic condition. During a Saturn transit, it may be beneficial to increase vitamins and minerals through food intake or by taking supplements of Saturn-ruled vitamins and minerals.

Saturn to the Sun affects health by lowering vitality and resistance. One may suffer colds or chills and poor circulation. Those that have been neglecting their health may encounter a difficult health problem during this transit that forces them to take responsibility for their bodies. Saturn is the reality principle, and the body cannot be ignored if one is hit with a health crisis.

Transiting Saturn to the Moon can affect the emotional health, resulting in great emotional pain. This transit can affect psychological health by forcing one to come to terms with such emotions as loneliness, alienation, depression and fear. These emotional problems must be dealt with because repressed (Saturn) emotions can manifest as physical problems.

Transiting Saturn to Mercury can manifest as respiratory problems, nerve related disorders and speech defects. There can be an overly pessimistic attitude which lowers resistance.

Transiting Saturn to Venus may manifest as a glandular disorder, dermatitis, kidney problems or throat problems.

Transiting Saturn to Mars can indicate the onset of a health disorder. It can also indicate an energy block; a muscle problem, difficulty with joints or bones, susceptibility to infection, broken bones or a blood disease.

Transiting Saturn to Jupiter could indicate diseases relating to arteriosclerosis, liver dysfunction, gallbladder problems or tension-related ailments.

Transiting Saturn to Saturn can indicate a crisis period where resistance is down and vitality is lowered. This is usually a testing period with heightened tension or stress. An increase of the B vitamins plus calcium and magnesium during this time may be of benefit.

Transiting Saturn to Uranus can be a time of increased tension. Bodily rhythm can be altered or inhibited, circulatory problems can result; in severe cases there can be heart block. With this transit there is a need to let go of the past and allow change. The more one resists, the more likely one is to develop a health problem.

Transiting Saturn to Neptune can indicate a chronic illness. This is a good time for a thorough medical checkup. This can be a time of anxiety and pessimism which lowers bodily resistance.

Transiting Saturn to Pluto can indicate health problems due to obsessive behavior or drive and overwork. There can be a health condition that limits one's lifestyle or a health crisis that forces one to evaluate one's current lifestyle.

Transits of Uranus

Transits from Uranus affect the health through spasm, accidents, circulatory problems, nerve-related problems and altered heartbeat.

Transiting Uranus to the Sun can affect cardiovascular health. Overly impulsive behavior can lead to an accident. There can be much tension and nervousness with erratic breathing and highs and lows in the vitality. There can be nervous strain and heart palpitations. Suppression of Uranian energy could lead to tension-related ailments and circulatory problems.

Uranus transiting the Moon can distort bodily rhythm in women. A person can be hypersensitive, exhibiting emotional ups and downs. Nerves can be overstrained. A person under Uranus Moon transits needs calming influences such as herbal teas that relax the nerves and quiet times to be alone.

Uranus transiting Mercury disturbs the equilibrium and can indicate extreme nervousness and mental tension. There can be headaches, tremors, spastic conditions or digestive difficulty.

Uranus transiting Venus can cause emotional tension, skin problems, circulatory disorders, malfunctioning glands and a difficulty in balancing the energies of the body.

Transiting Uranus to Mars can indicate metabolic disturbances, the possibility of an operation, accidents involving machinery, firearms or explosives, carelessness, or blood loss. Suppression of this energy, which should be used toward individual expression, can manifest as physical illness.

Uranus to Jupiter transits can indicate a release of inner strain or tension. Negatively, there can be spastic conditions in the body, intestinal disorders and illness due to wrong diet.

Uranus to Saturn transits can manifest as physical tension, strain, cardiovascular difficulties, psychosomatic illness, or nervous disorders. It is important to find some release of tension either through physical exercise or by making positive structural changes in the life.

Uranus transit to Uranus could manifest as nervousness and tension. Change must be dealt with appropriately; there can be a turning point in health for better or worse.

Uranus to Neptune transits can cause a lack of emotional balance and nervous sensitivity. There can be less stamina and vitality, confused perceptions, and altered states of consciousness. There can be unusual illnesses, decreased mental functions, problems due to drugs and much fatigue. This is a good time for a medical checkup.

Uranus to Pluto can indicate bodily transformation on a physical or psychological level. A person may become involved with consciousness raising techniques that put the individual more in touch with his or her body.

Transits of Neptune

Transits of Neptune can be especially difficult because with Neptune there can be something hidden or disguised, making diagnosis difficult. With a Neptune transit, a disease can be discovered which is already in an advanced state. Neptune transits affect the immune system and can lower vitality. These transits can cause a person to lose touch with reality—thus ignoring the needs of the body.

Neptune transits to the Sun may deplete vitality, cause anemia, create toxic reactions to drugs, increase water concentration in the cells and lower resistance to disease.

Neptune transiting the Moon can cause excess fluid in the bodily tissues, increased sensitively to drugs, a drug overdose, allergic reactions, a loss of grip on reality or nervous sensitivity and the possibility of a coma.

Neptune transiting Mercury indicates mental confusion, an oversensitivity to drugs, nervousness and anxiety or disease relating to the nervous system.

Neptune transiting Venus can cause weakened glands, a sugar imbalance in the bloodstream, a lack of body tone, and difficulties caused from overindulgence in sugar-laden foods.

Neptune transiting Mars can correlate with infections, a misuse of physical energy, less energy than usual, anemia and/or a blood disorder and increased sensitivity to drugs.

Neptune transiting Jupiter can indicate escapist tendencies, a lack of bodily tone and misdiagnosis. Harmon describes Neptune Jupiter combinations as involuntary trance, accidents with gas or fumes and drowning.[27]

Neptune transiting Saturn can indicate the beginning of a long term illness. Any minor health problems that develop under this transit should be carefully monitored as one is more prone to debility than usual. One may need more rest than usual at this time. This is a good time for a physical checkup.

Neptune transiting Uranus can affect the nerves and disturb bodily rhythms. There can be doubt and uncertainty which can result in escapist tendencies. At times there can be the feeling of losing one's grip on reality so recreational drugs should be avoided.

Transits of Neptune to Uranus or Uranus to Neptune can correlate with a coma.

Neptune transiting Neptune can be a time of insight and higher consciousness. One may turn to more holistic methods of healing. A person needs much time alone to sort through the emotional confusion that can accompany this transit.

Neptune transiting Pluto can indicate a hidden disease, a refusal to deal with the body, unhealthy cravings and general confusion. Positively, one may discover a therapy—psychological or physical—to help combat a health condition.

Transits of Pluto

Transits of Pluto can indicate bodily transformation—for better or for worse. There can be a psychological or physical rebirth—possibly brought on by a health crises. Problems with the reproductive, eliminative or endocrine systems of the body may develop. It is possible that hereditary problems may manifest under a Pluto transit. One may take drastic measures under a Pluto transit.

Pluto transiting the Sun can indicate swellings, changes in the cells and bodily transformation. A body that has been abused may break down with the resultant need for techniques that will build it up. A previously ill person may find positive bodily regeneration occurring at this time.

Pluto-Moon transits can correlate with emotional problems, digestive difficulties and allergic reactions. There can be a health disorder relating to females.

Pluto-Venus transits can correlate with abnormalities to the sex life, problems relating to females, venereal disease, or unusual skin growths such as warts, fungus or moles.

Pluto-Mars transits can manifest emotionally as anger and resentment or can indicate an accident. There can be a massive infection or problems with the reproductive or eliminative systems. Pluto-Mars transits can indicate excessive drive leading to physical exhaustion. This transit can indicate an organ transplant.

Pluto transiting Jupiter can be beneficial for improved health. Health therapies can be successful: there can be a positive regeneration of organs. This can be a good time to try a detoxifying diet to help clear up health problems—especially relating to cleansing of arteries or the colon.

Pluto to Saturn can indicate bodily transformation either for better or worse. There can be structural changes affecting the teeth, bones, skin or joints. There can be organ degeneration, cell changes, or a need to make drastic changes to improve the health.

Pluto transiting Uranus can bring dramatic change into the life that may or may not affect health. The sign Uranus tenants may be a clue to the health condition. This transit can indicate nervous conditions.

Pluto transiting Neptune may be a time of change on an emotional and physical level. There can be a bodily transformation that will be slow to develop. Increased spiritual awareness may cause a person to lose touch with physical necessities of the body or put one more in touch with the body.

Pluto transiting Pluto indicates a time of change as the new replaces the old. Previous neglect of the body can signify a health crises and a need to transform bad health habits to more healthful ones. Health problems from the past may become critical under this transit.

Combining Predictive Techniques in Assessing Severity and Duration of Illness

The preceding information on transits can be used as a guide to determine the severity of a health condition. The slower the transiting body moves the stronger will be its influence. Most difficult are stationary outer planet transits to a personal point—the most difficult being the retrograde period. This information is then combined with progressions and directions to give a more complete picture. Monthly lunar progressions can be used to describe one's emotional state—which can have a bearing on health. General health conditions can be observed by watching the aspects formed from the progressed Moon to natal and progressed planets. The progressed Moon conjunct the natal Ascendant can indicate a change in bodily health as well as a change in one's environment.

Solar arc directions are a further clue in determining health or severity of a disease. They are especially useful in combination with natal midpoints in giving more detailed information. With their approximate movement of five minutes a month, they make excellent timers. A condition can manifest itself or become more acute during the month a particular solar arc direction is exact. For example, solar arc Neptune aspecting natal Mars indicates toxicity and susceptibility to infection. The severity and duration of the condition depends on the other cosmic influences in operation at the time and the inclusion of personal points.

Eclipses, which are known as energizers, can also signify a health crisis. The effects of lunations are not as strong, but along with other indications could indicate a potential health problem. Determining the severity of the eclipse is dependant on aspects made to the eclipse point by other transiting planets and the location of the eclipse in the natal chart—an aspect to personal points being the most potent—conjunctions and oppositions the strongest. Using the prenatal eclipse point—the last eclipse occurring previous to birth—is another method for determining severity of disease. Transits, directions, progressions or an eclipse to that point have been known to trigger a health crises.

Combining Chart Analysis with Predictive Techniques

Using a step-by-step approach, three charts will be used and compared to determine severity and duration of disease. Chart C is that of a female with fibrocystic breast disease—three times a large breast lump was discovered and removed surgically—each time the lump was described as benign. Chart D is that of a female who was diagnosed as having cancer and who through chemotherapy and radiation treatment was cured. Chart E is that of a female who was diagnosed as having breast cancer and who subsequently passed away. A comparison of these three charts will show how medical astrology techniques can point out disease indicators and immunity and how by combining this information with predictive techniques, one may be able to determine the severity of the illness.

The steps presented in giving a health reading will be utilized in the following analyses. The first step is to examine the three charts for vitality and resistance to disease. We begin with an examination of the Sun and Moon as indicators of a person's vitality and general health.

Sun—Chart C

In Chart C, natal Sun is in Capricorn, a sign that is not considered robust but tends to longevity. The constitution can be weak in early life but gains strength as the person ages. Natal Sun is conjunct Mercury in a grand cross with Jupiter, Saturn and the Moon. Although Jupiter is out of orb to a

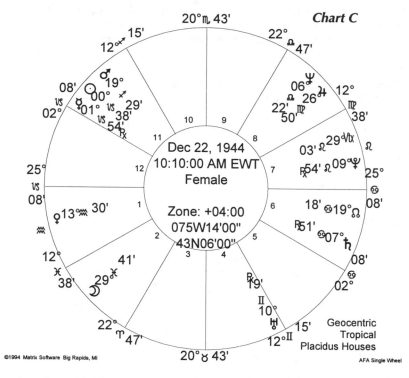

Chart C

20°♏ 43'

12°♐ 15'

♂ 19°
08' ☉ 00° ♐
02° ☿ 01° ♈ 29'
♈ 38'
54'
℞

22° ♎ 47'

♆
06° ♎ 26° ♃ 12°
22' 50' ♏ ♍ 38'

10   9

8

Dec 22, 1944
10:10:00 AM EWT
Female

Zone: +04:00
075W14'00"
43N06'00"

11

12

7

03' ♌ 29° ♍
℞ 54' ♌ 09° ♇ 25°
♋

6

18' ♋ 19° ☊ 08'
℞ 51' ♋ 07° ♄

25°
♑
08'

13°♒ 30'   1
♒

2

5

3   4

08'

12°
♓ 41'
38' ♓ 29°
☽

℞ 19'
♊ 10°

02° ♋

22°
♈ 47'

♅ 15'
12°♊

Geocentric
Tropical
Placidus Houses

20° ♉ 43'

©1994 Matrix Software Big Rapids, MI

AFA Single Wheel

conjunction with Neptune, Neptune is also involved with a grand cross with the Sun-Mercury conjunction, Saturn and the Moon. These aspects describe a person with lowered resistance, a weak constitution or lowered vitality, and one who is subject to nervous stress.

There is the possibility of sickness through excess and the possibility of a chronic health problem. There is a need for rest and relaxation to conserve the vital energies, a need for physical exercise and breathing exercises to stimulate the body, and a need to reduce exposure to overly stressful situations.

Despite these difficult aspects, the Sun is strengthened by an exact parallel with Mars. This strengthens the vitality and constitution and aids a sense of determination to the nature. The Sun is contraparallel Pluto which can add a regenerative quality to the constitution.

In checking relevant midpoint configurations, note Sun 00 Capricorn 38 widely square Mars/Saturn 28 Virgo/Pisces 40. This can weaken the vitality and cause poor health but at the same time, due to the nature of a Capricorn Sun, can give strong powers of endurance. The Sun is also semisquare/sesquiquadrate Jupiter/Saturn 17 Leo/Aquarius 20, which can cause inconstancy in the health. The Sun square Jupiter/Neptune 01 Aries/Libra 01 Aries/Libra 36 indicates a need to conserve energy. And the Sun semisquare/sesquiquadrate Moon/Mercury 15 Leo/Aquarius 48 can be indicative of female complaints such as breast tenderness and water retention prior to menstruation (suffered by client).

Moon—Chart C

An examination of the Moon finds it involved in the same configurations as the Sun. This would indicate a person with fluctuating health and a concern with health problems. The Moon is also critically placed at 29 Pisces 41. With its opposition to Neptune and square to Saturn, there is a need to deal realistically with emotions such as guilt, anger and jealousy. It is interesting that physical problems manifested in the breasts—the ruler of the breasts, Cancer, is doubly afflicted. Its ruler, the Moon, is in a critical degree and part of a grand cross and Saturn is in Cancer in the sixth house. Saturn's tenancy of a sign indicates a weak point in the body and its placement in the sixth house indicates a concern with health. It should be pointed out that Saturn in Cancer can also refer to digestive difficulties. Thus, it is not always easy to predict beforehand where a health disorder will manifest. Rather, one will be able to determine astrologically the reason a particular part of the body is affected.

The Moon at 29 Pisces 41 is at the Mars/Saturn midpoint at 28 Virgo/Pisces 40, indicating possible illness or a weak will; it is also semisquare/sesquiquadrate Mars/Neptune 12 Taurus/Scorpio 55—indicating possible nervous weakness, moodiness and an oversensitive nature.

Ascendant—Chart C

Like the Sun, the Ascendant is also in Capricorn. Davidson considers Capricorn to be the greatest resistor—a sign that gets stronger as it ages. As the person ages, the vital forces flow more readily throughout the body while at the same time, resisting disease.[28] The Ascendant is aided by a sextile from the Moon and a close trine from Jupiter, assisting the flow of the vital forces and giving protection. A close sesquiquadrate from Uranus to the Ascendant indicates that at times this flow will be erratic, and it is also descriptive of a person who can be hypersensitive and who needs to do her own thing in life. This can also be seen by unaspected Mars in Sagittarius. There can be bodily tension or stress-related illness as her strong Capricornian nature toward hard work and responsibility vies with the freedom-loving and rebellious nature of Uranus to the Ascendant and unaspected Mars in Sagittarius.

Contradictory energies such as these can manifest physically or emotionally in rebellious behavior, temper tantrums, antisocial behavior, depression, anxiety or lack of confidence. It is usually denial or repression as shown by the Saturn-Moon configuration that may manifest later as a physical problem, fixed signs being the most difficult.

Chart C's Ascendant at 25 Capricorn 08 is square Venus/Saturn at 25 Aries/Libra 40, indicating emotional inhibitions and separations from others.

Quadruplicity Emphasis—Chart C

An examination of the chart reveals the greatest difficulty in the cardinal quadruplicity. There is a cardinal grand cross with only the Moon out of sign. However, the Moon rules a cardinal sign. Using the point system, there are eighteen points in cardinal, four in fixed and ten in mutable. There is also an earth/water emphasis which, combined with the cardinal emphasis, is descriptive of the signs Cancer and Capricorn. These are all indications of health problems anatomically described by cardinal signs, which could be a difficulty in the area of the breasts. With Saturn in Cancer, there is an indication of poor blood supply to the breasts and possible hardening or obstruction.

Despite the apparent difficult aspects and affliction in cardinal signs, the planets involved fall either in succedent or cadent houses, thus minimizing the health risk. There are no planets on angles and only minor affliction to the angles. The Uranus aspect to the Ascendant more likely describes Chart C's erratic nature and rebelliousness in early years; the semisquare of Neptune to the Midheaven can indicate confused goals or a misguided direction. What is most interesting is that with the Sun and Mercury conjunct the twelfth house cusp, Saturn in the sixth, and Neptune, natural ruler of the twelfth house, semisquare the Midheaven, Chart C has spent most of her working years in a health field working for doctors or working as a technician in a hospital.

Midpoints—Chart C

In examining the health midpoints we find Sun/Moon, Mars/Uranus and Mars/Pluto unaffected. The Midheaven at 20 Scorpio 43 is square Saturn/Neptune at 22 Leo/Aquarius 06, a configuration indicating illness. Jupiter at 26 Virgo 50 semisquare/sesquiquadrate Mars/Neptune 12 Taurus/Scorpio 55 can weaken vitality. Venus at 13 Aquarius 30 square Mars/Neptune 12 Taurus/Scorpio 55 and semisquare/sesquiquadrate Mars/Saturn 28 Virgo/Pisces 40 indicates the possibility of infection and health problems in areas ruled by Taurus and Libra, as well as a difficulty in balancing the energies of the body. For a complete health reading, one would examine all midpoint configurations.

Resistance to Disease—Chart C

Chart C's Capricorn influence adds strength to the body while Mars, unaspected in Sagittarius, is strengthened by its position as the most elevated planet in the chart. There is the ability to attack disease and burn off toxins. Pluto at 9 Leo 54 is semisquare/sesquiquadrate Sun/Mars 25 Gemini/Sagittarius 03, giving the ability to fight disease and burn off toxins. The emphasis of cardinal and mutable signs over fixed ones means A does not hold onto illness. A Scorpio influence is an aid to throwing off disease and Chart C's Midheaven is in Scorpio. The chart has a grand trine in air which also has a protective influence as air is a good conductor of energy. Despite chart indications of possible health problems, there is the ability to resist and throw off illness.

The speed or slowness of the metabolism is examined next. Chart C's Sun-Saturn opposition slows up the metabolism and can indicate a tendency toward alkalinity. Sun square Neptune also weakens the metabolism. There are, however, mitigating factors to the Sun-Saturn and Sun-Neptune aspects. Sun parallel Mars and contraparallel Pluto increases metabolic activity, thus increasing the fight against disease. Unaspected Mars in Sagittarius with its strong fiery nature increases metabolic activity, thus aiding recovery.

Sun—Chart D

Chart D contains an angular Sun in Gemini conjunct and parallel the Ascendant. This is a good indication for longevity and vitality. The Sun is considered strong in air as it aids the vitality and constitution. The trine of the Sun to Jupiter further increases the vitality and adds a protective influence to

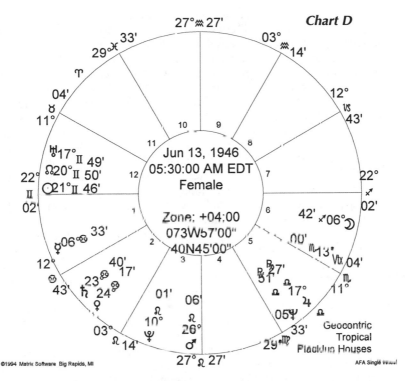

27°≈ 27'

29°♓ 33'

♈

03°≈ 14'

04'

12°

♉

♑

11°

43'

10   9

11

8

♅17° ♊ 49'

Jun 13, 1946

22°

☊20° ♊ 50'

05:30:00 AM EDT

7

22°

☉21°♊ 46'

Female

♊

♐

02'

12

02'

☿06°♋ 33'

Zone: +04:00

6

42' ♐06°☽

073W57'00"

1

00'

40N45'00"

♏13' Vtx 04'

12°

2

3   4

5

♏

40' 17'

♃27'

11°

♋

23°♋

♎17°

43'

♄ 24°♋

01'

06'

♃

05♇

Geocentric

♀

♌

♎

Tropical

03°

10°

26°

33'

Placidus Houses

♌14' ♇

♂

29♍

27° ♌ 27'

©1994 Matrix Software Big Rapids, MI

AFA Single Wheel

the life. The semisextile of the Sun to Saturn could slightly weaken the constitution while the conjunction of Uranus to the Sun can give an inconstancy to the vitality and constitution and also contributes to personality quirks—the need for freedom, mobility and individual action—needs that if not met could manifest as physical illness or emotional problems. Sun is also parallel Uranus which reinforces the conjunction. The Sun's parallel to Pluto gives regenerative power.

Chart D's Sun at 21 Gemini 46 semisquare/sesquiquadrate Moon/Neptune 06 Taurus/Scorpio 17 can indicate weakened female organs and a delicate constitution. However, the Sun = Jupiter/MC 22 Gemini/Sagittarius 27 adds to a healthy physique.

Moon—Chart D

An examination of the Moon shows fluctuating conditions of health. Moon in the sixth house indicates a concern with health. The quincunx from Mercury to the Moon can indicate some conflict between the intellect and emotional expression, but this should not adversely affect health. It can be descriptive of a sensitive nervous system made worse through stressful working conditions. The Moon is sesquiquadrate Chart D's Saturn-Venus conjunction, indicating emotional inhibitions, lack of confidence, difficulty in emotional fulfillment and feelings of alienation. With the strong second and sixth house connection and with the Moon's rulership of the second house, health problems could be

49

related to stress in earnings and working conditions.

Chart D's lymphoma was discovered in her lower abdomen. Several tumors of the lymph glands were discovered in her lower abdomen with a metastasis to the ovaries. Subsequent radiation treatment caused Chart D to stop ovulating and the menstrual cycle ceased. Ebertin gives Moon-Venus as menstruation. Carter gives rulership of the ovaries to Venus and Cancer. The Moon is generally believed to rule the menstrual cycle and afflictions to the Moon could indicate a disturbance in the cycle. Harmon gives Venus as rulership over the ovaries. Heindel gives the Moon for the ovaries; Daath gives Venus for the ovaries. Other medical astrologers give Scorpio for the ovaries. In Chart D's chart there are no afflictions in Scorpio and its rulers, Mars and Pluto, are well aspected. However, Scorpio is on the cusp of the sixth house receiving a square from Pluto. The Vertex is in Scorpio conjunct the sixth house cusp and afflicted from a square by Pluto. This could indicate a fatalistic transformation affecting fixed signs and could be a health matter—sixth house Vertex. Tumors can be indicated by fixed signs, especially the Taurus-Scorpio axis. The influence of Pluto is consistent with malignancy.

A case can also be made for assigning the sign Cancer to the ovaries. Note the Moon, ruler of Cancer, is afflicted by a Venus-Saturn conjunction in Cancer; Saturn doubly afflicts the sign Cancer and with its conjunction to Venus, disturbs the balancing energies of the body. Mercury is afflicted in the sign Cancer by a square from Neptune and a quincunx to the Moon. And the Saturn-Venus conjunction is further afflicted by Jupiter. Jupiter, when afflicted, can indicate proliferation—thus describing the metastasis to the ovaries. Using this chart, a case can be made for rulership of the ovaries to be either Scorpio or Cancer; needless to say, more research needs to be done in this area. However, remaining with Scorpio's rulership of reproductive processes, the strength of the Vertex in Scorpio can describe the twist of fate that prevents Chart D from being able to conceive.

In examining midpoints involving the Moon, the Moon at 6 Sagittarius 43 is semisquare/sesquiquadrate Mars/Uranus at 21 Cancer/Capricorn 57, which can signify an operation on a woman. Chart D's cancer was discovered during what was to be a simple gynecological operation.

Ascendant—Chart D

Chart D's Gemini Ascendant is a good conductor of energy. It is further strengthened by the conjunction of the Sun and the trine from Jupiter. The conjunction of Uranus to the Ascendant adds a note of restlessness or unpredictability to the personality; she can become high strung or nervous under stress. The Uranus-Ascendant conjunction combined with the mutability of Gemini indicates that the energy flow throughout the body is not always constant. Chart D may suffer from nervous excitability to the point of depleting the vital energies. This Uranus conjunction to the Ascendant is also reinforced by being parallel to the Ascendant. Pluto, closely parallel the Ascendant, describes a person who is innately aware of the need for continual regeneration and who could go through a bodily transformation. It is interesting to note that Chart D has always felt a strong urge to be on a spiritual path.

With the close conjunction of the Sun to the Ascendant, any midpoints involving the Sun also include the Ascendant. Midpoints relevant to health include the Ascendant at 22 Gemini 02 semisquare/sesquiquadrate Moon/Neptune at 6 Taurus/Scorpio 17, which can describe a sick person.

Quadruplicity Emphasis—Chart D

In examining the quadruplicities by the point system, one notes an emphasis in mutability and cardinality. There are no heavy afflictions to angles. Though Uranus aspects the Ascendant, it almost exactly trines Jupiter, adding a protective influence. Mars aspecting an angle indicates acute illness or infections which can be the body's way of burning off toxins. Other planetary afflictions are found in succedent or cadent houses, making the disease less of a life threatening situation than if these planets were in angular houses or afflicting angles. Although there are planets in earth houses, there are no planets in earth signs, which can describe an impractical person who neglects basic health habits. This, combined with a strong air emphasis, can indicate someone who lives in her head and doesn't like to deal with mundane matters. Chart D has planets in water, which help flush out toxins in the body, and planets in fire, which aid her in fighting disease. The lack of an emphasis in fixed signs is a good indication of an acute condition. The mutable emphasis in the chart brings in the possibility of a disturbance to the lymphatic system. As stated earlier, the cancer affected the lymph glands in the abdominal area.

Midpoints—Chart D

In examining the health midpoints, Pluto at 10 Leo 01 is at the midpoint of Mars/Saturn at 9 Leo/Aquarius 53. This could indicate a disturbance involving Pluto's rulership of the reproductive system. Chart D's Sun/Moon 14 Virgo/Pisces 14 conjoins Mars/Neptune 15 Virgo/Pisces 58, which could indicate toxicity in the body. And Chart D's Saturn 23 Cancer 40 is midpoint Sun/Mars 23 Cancer/Capricorn 56, which lowers vitality and can cause bodily weakness

Resistance to Disease—Chart D

Chart D's metabolic activity is strengthened by Mars in Leo closely conjunct the IC. The semisextile from Saturn to Mars has an orb of two degrees, indicating the possibility of Saturn sometimes hindering Mars in fighting disease. However, as Mars by placement is stronger than Saturn, it is unlikely that this aspect has much influence. The Sun-Uranus conjunction can disturb metabolic activity. But there is an emphasis in mutable and air signs which increases the metabolic rate. The Sun rising, the Moon in fire (Sagittarius) and Mars in fire and angular are all indications of increased metabolic activity and the ability to burn off harmful toxins.

Davidson discusses the importance of estimating the relative strength of Mars and Saturn to determine whether a person can fight disease.

"A patient with an angular Mars very strong slips into acute conditions consistently, but there's a purifying process. Mars is fight whether it is psychological or whether it is physiological ."[29]

It has already been determined that Chart D's Mars is stronger by placement than her Saturn. The emphasis in fire and air also helps fight disease and the mutable emphasis is an aid in throwing off disease.

51

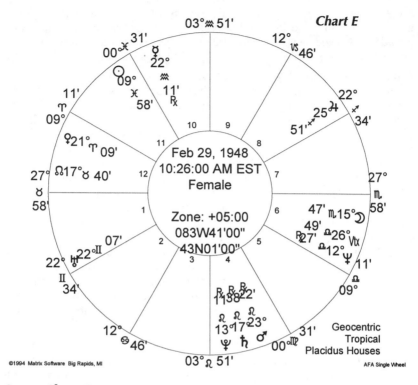

Chart E

03°≈51'

00°ᛣ31'

12°ᛣ46'

☿22°≈

☉09°≈

)(58' 11' ℞

11'
09° ♈

♀21°♈09'

22°♃34'
25°♃
51'♐

10   9

Feb 29, 1948
10:26:00 AM EST
Female

8

27° Ω17°♉40' 12

Zone: +05:00
083W41'00"
43N01'00"

7

27°
♏58'

♉
58'

1   2   5   6

47'♏15°)
49'
℞27' ♎26°Vtx
♎12°♇
11'

22°♊
♅22°♊07'

3   4

♎
09°

♊
34'

℞1138°22'
Ω Ω Ω
13°17°23°
♇ ♄ ♂

12°
♋46'

31' Geocentric
00°♏ Tropical
Placidus Houses

03°Ω51'

©1994 Matrix Software Big Rapids, MI   AFA Single Wheel

Sun—Chart E

Chart E contains a Sun in Pisces widely trine the Moon and closely quincunx Neptune. One would expect a Sun-Moon trine to be beneficial in terms of health, bestowing vitality and strengthening the constitution. However, the Sun is weakly placed in Pisces, a sign of lowered resistance and considered weakest in vitality and strength unless counterbalanced by other chart factors. In Chart E's case, the Sun is further weakened by being quincunx its ruler, Neptune. Any hard aspect of Neptune to the Sun depletes the vital forces, disturbs the constitution, causes weakness and can indicate a prolonged healing time. Note also Neptune's tenancy of the sixth house. The Vertex is also found in the sixth house and is sesquiquadrate the Sun. Venus, the chart ruler and ruler of the sixth house is widely conjunct the Antivertex. This is an affliction in cardinal signs. Cancer, which rules the breasts, is a cardinal sign.

The emphasis on the Pisces Sun afflicted by its ruler Neptune can describe a person who has difficulty in withstanding disease. This combination can also describe a person who has difficulty in dealing with reality, who uses avoidance techniques and who is easily influenced by others. Chart E's main purpose in life was the spiritual path. She ignored her condition and even ran out of a hospital minutes before an exploratory operation because she didn't like the looks of the attendants. It was around four months after discovering the lump in her breast that she finally allowed a doctor to operate under the condition

52

that he would do nothing until he spoke to her. She was then told that she had a malignant tumor that had grown too large to be surgically removed. The cancer was spreading toward the abdomen. A radiation implant was suggested. Chart E rejected this idea, convinced by friends in her spiritual group that radiation could be worse than cancer. She entered a clinic that used holistic methods to cure breast cancer. Chart E even stated to this author that she didn't care if she died as long as she didn't have to suffer. The clinic was unable to cure her; she suffered terribly and subsequently entered a hospital where she passed on.

Moon—Chart E

An examination of Chart E's Moon shows it to be in the fixed sign Scorpio, involved in a fixed T-square with Mercury at one end and a Mars, Saturn Pluto conjunction at the other end. This is a particularly difficult combination and indicates poor conditions of health. Note the Moon is afflicted in Scorpio; at one time Chart E had colitis, a bowel disorder. Afflictions to the ruler of the breasts in a fixed sign can indicate tumor formation, as fixed signs can indicate aggregation. Note again the Taurus-Scorpio axis involved in tumor formation. And not only is the T-square fixed, but all the angles are in fixed signs. Although fixed signs can indicate endurance, they can also describe a holding on or a stubborn personality who needs to learn how to let go. The Moon in Scorpio, usually an eliminative sign, is held back by the square from Saturn. This Scorpio Moon can describe a person who suppressed her emotional needs causing them to fester within the body until they erupted into a physical ailment. The emphasis on the fixed quadruplicity combined with a difficulty in eliminating toxins from the body resulted in a tumor. The Moon is further afflicted by a contraparallel from Saturn. Chart E was known to hold back her anger and took a lot of abuse at work—Moon afflicted in the sixth house of work. She had a dream in which it was stated to her that the reason she got the tumor was due to her inability to express her anger at her co-workers. She was working as a bartender at the time of her illness—Neptune in the sixth house.

The combination of Mars, Saturn and Pluto afflicting the Moon can indicate difficulties with the breasts, pain and inflammation, tumor formation, retention of toxins and chronic disease. Jupiter sesquiquadrate Pluto may describe the spread of the cancer to her abdomen, also ruled by the sign Cancer.

Chart E's Moon 15 Scorpio 47 is square Saturn/Pluto 15 Leo/Aquarius 25, which Ebertin describes as "the tragic destiny of a woman."[30] Chart E was 35 when she died. Chart E's Moon is also square Uranus/Neptune at 17 Leo/Aquarius 17, which can indicate attacks of debility.

Ascendant—Chart E

Chart E's Ascendant is in the earth sign Taurus, a sign not considered a good conductor of energy. Taurus needs to avoid toxins as it has a tendency to retain toxins; otherwise it can be a sign of endurance. The square of Mars to the Ascendant could increase the flow of bodily energy, but Mars is hampered by its conjunction to Saturn. Mercury's square to the Ascendant could indicate nervousness and a need to learn how to relax. Health could worsen under stress and Chart E was under a lot of stress at her job and also worked long hours.

Jupiter's quincunx to the Ascendant indicates a need to be more disciplined. Neptune's sesquiquadrate to the Ascendant weakens the flow of vital energies throughout the body and reinforced Chart E's sense of dreaminess, lack of resistance and influence by others.

The Ascendant at 27 Taurus 57 is at the midpoint of both Sun/Saturn at 28 Taurus/Scorpio 48 and Sun/Pluto at 26 Taurus/Scorpio 34, which could manifest as illness, environmental separations and cell transformation.

Quadruplicity Emphasis—Chart E

An examination of the quadruplicities by points places an emphasis in the fixed quadruplicity. As stated previously, the fixed signs can accumulate toxins which can aggregate into tumors. The Mars-Saturn-Pluto conjunction is made more difficult by being in an angular house and retrograde. In fact, Chart E's chart contains five retrograde planets—retrograde planets being considered more difficult in terms of health. Mercury, also a part of the fixed T-square, is also in an angular house. Pluto is widely conjunct the IC, thus emphasizing its ability for cell replication. As stated earlier, Neptune retrograde, afflicts the Ascendant from the sixth house. Uranus afflicts the Midheaven by sesquiquadrate and in turn afflicts Jupiter. This would be a mutable affliction in succedent houses and could indicate a weakened immune system. We also find the Nodes in Taurus-Scorpio in the sixth and twelfth houses—connection with hospitals. And it should also be noted that the Mars-Saturn-Pluto conjunction falls in the fourth house, the natural house of the sign Cancer, ruler of the breasts and stomach.

Midpoints—Chart E

An examination of the health midpoints reveals the following: Neptune 12 Libra 27 square Sun/Moon 12 Cancer/Capricorn 53. This can lower vitality and weaken the constitution. It can also indicate a lowered immune response. The Midheaven 3 Aquarius 51 semisquare/sesquiquadrate Mars/Neptune 17 Virgo/Pisces 54, indicating a weak or sick person, possibly with a lack of the drive needed to deal with difficult problems. And Chart E's Jupiter 25 Sagittarius 51 conjunct Sun/Neptune 26 Gemini/Sagittarius 12, also indicating a weak vitality and constitution.

Chart E's angular Mars and Pluto can describe a person who gets acute diseases and who can burn off toxins. However, Saturn 17 Leo 38 = Mars/Pluto 18 Leo/Aquarius 16 and is also afflicted and angular, describing the lack of consistency in fighting off disease. The strength of Saturn, combined with indicators at the time of the disease, allowed the disease to go on. The transformation, represented by Pluto, was toward cell replication, consistent with cancer and further aggravated by the sesquiquadrate from Jupiter. This, plus the strong fixed emphasis (especially fixed signs on all the angles) all contributed to the worsening of her condition.

Resistance to Disease—Chart E

Metabolic activity is weakened by the quincunx of Neptune to the Sun. The emphasis of planets in fire signs should help the metabolism but there are indications to the contrary. Taurus rising lowers the metabolic rate, and the emphasis in fixed signs also lowers the metabolic rate. Pluto angular, usually an aid to metabolic activity, is hindered by its conjunction to Saturn. Medically, Saturn impedes or slows down the sign it tenants or the planets it aspects. And, as stated above, Saturn is also conjunct the Mars/Pluto midpoint, a combination indicating a severe illness.

Examples from Charts C, D, and E will be used to illustrate how severity and duration of illness can be seen using predictive techniques.

Determining Severity and Duration of Disease:

A's first health crisis occurred on September 13, 1979 when surgery revealed a very large breast cyst. The cyst was removed and found to be benign. On August 22, 1979, an eclipse in 29 Leo 01 fell on Chart C's Vertex in the seventh house. In assessing health, this could indicate a difficulty in the fixed quadruplicity since the Vertex is in Leo. Fixed signs can indicate tumor formation, but as will be seen, there was no threat to the life. Transiting Jupiter was applying by three degrees to a conjunction with the Vertex. Also by transit was Sun square Mars and Mercury square Mars on September 12, and Venus trine the Ascendant on September 13. Although Mars can signify operations, these are not malefic transits. Interestingly, during each health crisis Venus was transiting to Jupiter—in this case by conjunction on September 14. Natal Jupiter tenants Chart C's eighth house, a house which can describe a crisis situation; natal Jupiter is sesquiquadrate natal Venus. Ebertin describes Venus-Jupiter as "the hormone circulation within the body, also hormone metabolism, the glands dealing with internal secretion..."[31] Fibrocystic breast disease is described by Rothenberg as "a glandular upset resulting in the formation of many cysts in the breasts of women ..."[32]

Progressed Sun at 5 Aquarius 58 was applying to a trine of natal and progressed Neptune. Sun-Neptune trines are very protective and although not exact in September 1979, the direction is toward improved health. Solar arc directed Ascendant at 00 Pisces 28 was applying by sextile to natal Sun, another indication of good health. Solar arc directed Mars at 24 Capricorn 50 was also applying to a conjunction to the Ascendant, an indication of improved vitality. From the above it can be seen that despite the potential for breast problems as shown in the natal chart, the predictive techniques showed no complications. A was diagnosed as having fibrocystic breast disease and at that time began to gather information on her condition so as to prevent a recurrence.

However, on June 10, 1980 a second breast cyst was discovered and removed. A cycle of transiting Uranus sesquiquadrate Chart C's natal Saturn had begun in December 1979. This usually is an aspect of physical tension. However, natal Saturn is in Chart C's sixth house in the sign of Cancer, which rules the breasts, and Saturn is the ruler of the chart and of Chart C's Sun. Saturn rules calcification. A problem affecting work or health might be expected with this aspect. Transiting Neptune was conjunct natal Mars beginning in January 1979 and reached exactitude in May 1979 and November 1979, with the transit approximately twenty-five minutes off in September 1980. This could have indicated a toxic condition in the body affecting both the September 13, 1979 and June 10, 1980 episodes. Tumors can form like pimples, enclosing toxic material. Mars-Neptune can also indicate abuse of the body, which perhaps lowered resistance. On June 9, transiting Sun was opposite Mars. On June 10, transiting Venus was square natal Jupiter.

It should be pointed out that prior to the first surgery, Pluto began applying to a square of the true North Node at 18 Cancer 32 in Chart C's sixth house. It was exact in December 1978, March 1979, and September 1979. Although not necessarily a health axis, this is an affliction again in the sign ruling the breasts. However, on June 10, 1980, the second surgery, Jupiter was semisquare the true North Node—a positive influence. In September 1979, after the first surgery, Saturn began applying to a square of natal Mars. This can indicate a health crisis, but the transit was not exact during the second surgery. The cyst removed during the second surgery was smaller than the one removed the previous September and was also found to be benign.

A third cyst was surgically removed on July 9, 1981. At that time transiting Uranus 26 Scorpio 22 was separating from a sextile to natal Jupiter, transiting Venus was applying to an opposition of natal Venus, and transiting Venus was semisquare natal Jupiter. Prior to this date, transiting Saturn squared natal Saturn—in December 1980 and March 1981. The cycle ended in August 1981. In those same months Jupiter was squaring natal Saturn by transit. Of themselves, none of these transits are life threatening. Jupiter square Saturn can be an indication of tension or stress. Saturn square Saturn can indicate a lowering of vitality and resistance and can describe a critical situation. There was a need to deal with the cause of these breast cysts. Thus, the Saturn square forced (Saturn) Chart C to assess her diet and other health practices so as to prevent further health crises. Again, Saturn, Chart C's chart ruler and ruler of her Sun, plus Saturn's tenancy of the sixth house, all contributed to this health crisis. In July 1981, progressed Sun at 7 Aquarius 50 was quincunx natal Saturn—again a need for reassessment in health matters. Solar arc directed Saturn at 15 Leo 03 was at the midpoint of Sun/Moon at 15 Leo/Aquarius 09, six minutes applying—another indication of chronic illness or lowered vitality and resistance to disease. Neptune by solar arc at 13 Scorpio 33 was also separating from a square to natal Venus. This could indicate toxic blood and a lowering of bodily tone.

From the preceding, the possibility of a health crisis can be seen but there were no indications of a threat to the life or any indication of a health crisis of long duration. A has a tendency to form fibroid tumors in the breast, but natal chart indicators show a person who, although having to deal with health problems, has the ability to fight and resist disease. And, as seen from the predictive methods used, there was a need to pay attention to health but this was combined with protective cosmic influences as well as short-term influences.

In the case of Chart D, it was during a routine gynecological examination on July 12, 1977 that a tumor was discovered. On July 11, transiting Mars was square natal Mars, fixed and angular. Neptune at 13 Sagittarius 53, separating by transit (retrograde), was square Sun/Moon at 14 Virgo/Pisces 14, which can indicate a weakened body. On July 15, 1977, x-rays confirmed the presence of a mass in the lower abdomen. On July 25, 1977, transiting Saturn was equal Chart D's Mars/Pluto at 18 Leo 03. This can be an indication of a serious health condition. Note Mars and Pluto both rule the reproductive system. There was no retrograde motion of Saturn over this midpoint. The progressed Sun at 21 Cancer 23 was applying to a conjunction of Mars/Uranus at 21 Cancer/Capricorn 57. This axis can indicate surgery, and Chart D did have two operations over the course of a year.

The first operation was performed on August 4, 1977 when several tumors of the lymph glands were discovered in Chart D's lower abdomen. Transiting Jupiter was separating by forty minutes from a sextile to natal Mars, which can be a protective combination. On August 6, 1977, transiting Jupiter was trine Chart D's Midheaven, affording more protection. However, the progressed Moon at 23 Capricorn 01 was opposing natal Saturn during August 1977. Saturn rules Chart D's eighth house—crisis and possible threat to the life. Natal Saturn is conjunct Chart D's Venus in Cancer, both in hard aspect to the Moon. Recall the earlier discussion of this combination being involved with the reproductive system and Chart D's inability to conceive. R.C. Davison describes progressed Moon-Saturn as affecting health through "accumulated waste matter in parts of the body ruled by the signs in which the Moon and Saturn are placed and by the signs opposite."[33]

On September 5, 1977, a second operation was performed which confirmed that Chart D had cancer. Transiting Venus at 10 Leo 01 was conjunct natal Pluto and Mars/Saturn at 9 Leo 53. There could be possible glandular disorders.

Chart D began radiation treatment on September 29, 1977. The treatment continued until November 4, 1977. When the treatments began, transiting Uranus was square Chart D's Mars/Saturn at 9 Leo/Aquarius 53. Uranus is the likely ruler of radiation and Mars/Saturn is considered a disease axis. However, this was the last transit of Uranus to this midpoint, so although the transit was exact on September 28, 1977, it may have had more to do with the overall situation of sudden illness or danger to the life. Also, on September 28, transiting Saturn began its cycle of a conjunction to natal Mars. This transit was exact again in February and June 1978. This was certainly a frustrating time requiring patience, and this planetary combination can also indicate endurance during a difficult time. Of interest is the fact that this Saturn-Mars cycle coincided very closely with the duration of the disease. The fact that it was life threatening is indicated by Saturn afflicting an angular Mars. This angular Mars is unafflicted natally except for the semisextile from Saturn conjunct Venus, which weakens it slightly. On September 30, 1977, Uranus made its last transiting square to Chart D's Pluto. The cycle began in December 1976 and was exact again in April 1977. Natal Pluto rules the sixth house of health but it is well aspected and cadent. However, it does reinforce the connection to the reproductive organs with Scorpio on the sixth house cusp and Pluto ruling reproduction. This transit can indicate a period of transformation, reform, and crisis. Also, on October 21, 1977, transiting Neptune completed its square to Chart D's Sun/Moon at 14 Virgo/Pisces 14.

Chart D began chemotherapy on November 17, 1977. On November 18, 1977, transiting Uranus was conjunct the natal Vertex, which is conjunct the sixth house cusp in Scorpio. The transit was exact again in June 1978 and ended in August 1978. Uranus can sometimes indicate a miraculous cure or could be indicative of the help from the radiation treatments. Chemotherapy is ruled by Neptune since it involves chemicals, but the last significant Neptune transit was the square to Sun/Moon on October 21.

On October 28, 1977, Pluto by transit was conjunct Chart D's natal Chiron at 14 Libra 54. Chiron is a planetoid that is sometimes prominent in the charts of health professionals and may be aspected during a health crisis. The transit occurred again in April and August 1978. Certainly, a health crisis was occurring as well as a transformation because, as stated earlier, the radiation treatments destroyed Chart D's ability to conceive.

Saturn by transit was conjunct Chart D's IC on October 12, 1977 and was also conjunct the IC in February and July 1978. Saturn can indicate chronic and long term ailments and its conjunction to the IC, along with the other factors, can indicate a life threatening situation.

When Chart D's cancer was discovered, progressed Mars at 14 Virgo 02 was applying to a conjunction of Sun/Moon at 14 Virgo/Pisces 14. This could describe the operations and may also describe the body fighting off the cancer. Chart D's tumors were discovered on July 12, 1977. On July 9 and 10, 1977, Jupiter was conjunct Chart D's Sun conjunct Ascendant configuration. Jupiter remained by transit in Chart D's first house until the middle of June 1978. By July 1978, Chart D's tumors had disappeared. There has been no reoccurrence of the cancer and Chart D has been in good health since that time.

The predictive techniques employed have shown the potential for a life threatening situation and for a health crisis requiring time before recovery. Jupiter's tenancy of Chart D's first house during the entire time of the illness seems more than a coincidence. And one of the meanings of Uranus transiting Mars/Saturn described previously is, according to Ebertin, "intervention by Higher Power or by Providence".[34] For those astrologers who think of Jupiter as a cosmic protector, its transit of Chart D's first house along with Chart D's ability to fight disease, as shown by her natal chart, gave her the ability to regain her health. As for duration, note also the cyclic dates of the transits as they correspond with the length of the disease.

We now turn to Chart E's chart, utilizing predictive techniques to indicate severity and duration of disease. In June 1983 C began complaining of a painful breast lump. During that month, Pluto began a retrograde transit of Chart E's Vertex at 26 Libra 49, which falls in her sixth house. In July 1983 Pluto was stationery direct on the Vertex, within minutes of exactitude. Pluto had made its first conjunction to the Vertex on October 19, 1982. This might be seen as a fatalistic situation dealing with work and health in which a transformation would occur. There were a great many difficulties involving Chart E's job during that time, but obviously it was a health crises that transformed her life. Since the Vertex is considered an angle and Pluto is a malefic, it is a life threatening combination. And as stated earlier, retrograde stations can worsen a situation. A computer readout of Chart E's solar arcs show solar arc directed Neptune square natal Saturn on July 23, 1983. This is a major health axis and a situation that worsened.

Although not life threatening, transiting Uranus was sesquiquadrate natal Venus first in December 1982, then in June 1983, and completed the cycle on

October 3, 1983. This brings in Venus' possible rulership of breast problems. And Uranus to Venus can indicate a disturbance in the equilibrium of the body. Venus rules her sixth house of health in Libra, a cardinal sign, again bringing in the cardinal axis and the cardinal sign Cancer, the more likely ruler of the breasts. Venus is also her chart ruler so the transit from Uranus can indicate a disturbance to the physical body.

In 1983, Saturn by transit squared Chart E's Midheaven/IC axis. Although usually associated with a professional or domestic crisis or hard work, this transit can be described as a malefic afflicting an angle. The transit occurred in January 1983 and March 1983, with the cycle ending on October 2, 1983. This transit also brings in the fixed quadruplicity associated with tumor formation.

On June 11, 1983 an eclipse at 19 Gemini 43 fell on Chart E's natal Uranus at 22 Gemini 07. Uranus rules her Midheaven/IC axis. It was this month that the tumor suddenly appeared.

As previously mentioned, Chart E did not deal realistically with her health problem. On August 8, 1983, the lunation fell on her Pluto in her fourth house. This is an angular Pluto and co-rules her sixth house of health and angular seventh house. Again, another Pluto influence and the involvement of fixed signs are seen. By the time Chart E allowed a doctor to operate on her in September 1983, it was found that she had a large malignant breast tumor—too large to be removed surgically. Chart E refused to have a radiation implant and left her home in October 1983 for treatment in a holistic clinic. A September 22, 1983 computer readout shows progressed Moon sesquiquadrate progressed Neptune. This combination can indicate self-deception, a difficulty in facing up to life's problems and a weakened body. On October 20, progressed Moon was sesquiquadrate natal Neptune, a continuation of this condition. On October 6, 1983 a lunation fell on Chart E's Neptune in her sixth house, thus weakening her condition and possibly describing her reluctance to deal realistically with her condition, as well as her belief that it didn't matter if she died as long as she didn't have to suffer.

Chart E was not helped by the clinic and left there to stay with her mother, who lived in another state. There were no helpful cosmic influences. A cycle of transiting Saturn square natal Pluto began December 23, 1983 and ended in September 1984. Saturn's conjunction by transit to her Moon began on January 28, 1984 and continued throughout 1984. Neptune by semisquare transited the natal Moon on February 13, 1984, the cycle continuing throughout that year. On February 23, 1984, transiting Saturn began a retrograde station on Chart E's true South Node at 16 Scorpio 27—four minutes off exactitude—in the sixth house of health. Chart E died February 28, 1984 while hospitalized.

Earlier explanations have described Chart E's propensity for health problems and the possibility of breast disease. Predictive techniques showed no relief of her health crisis. In fact, had Chart E not died in February 1984, one would have expected the condition to remain chronic throughout much of 1984 due to the Saturn transits. Although the sixth house was involved in this and previous chart analyses, it is the presence of malefics afflicting angles or planets on angles in combination with cosmic influences at the time of an illness that constitutes the greatest threat to the life. The inclusion of the sixth house is one more factor to take into consideration.

It will never be known if Chart E could have been saved had she either acted more quickly or chosen more conventional methods of treatment. Perhaps her will to live was not strong enough. Of the three charts studied in this section, her chart had the least resistance to disease and the greatest propensity toward tumor formation. Her fixed T-square was especially difficult and fell mostly in angular houses. Based on predictive techniques and the fact that both had cancer, both Charts D and E were involved in life threatening situations. However, Chart D had an enormous ability to fight disease and more beneficial cosmic influences at the time of her illness to help counteract the more difficult influences. In Chart E's case, there were no beneficial influences to counteract the difficult influences that were in operation during the course of her disease. A final note in the case of Chart C: Although there was always the possibility of her having a severe health problem, cosmic influences at the time of her health crisis were rather mild or non-existent.

In analyzing severity and duration of disease it is the combination of the natal chart along with the predictive techniques utilized that determine the possible duration of the disease and its final outcome. One must first follow the steps used in analyzing a chart for health; then one must combine this information with the predictive information. And no matter what the medical astrologer sees, unless the medical astrological is also a physician, it is his or her duty to describe the planetary action as seen in the chart and during the time of a health crisis and direct the person to the appropriate medical practitioner. One cannot predict with 100 percent accuracy the duration of a disease nor should one try to. Hopefully, the client will seek a holistically oriented doctor who could work with the medical astrologer, thus combining the best of both fields.

The remainder of this book includes six more case studies of persons suffering with various ailments as well as a final chapter on homeopathy.

Chapter Four

Case Studies

Chart F—An Acute Myocardial Infarction

Chart F is that of a victim (female) of two heart attacks. Chart F's Sun is posited in Pisces— a sign generally considered to be weak in bodily strength. It is also part of a yod formation with Pluto as the focal point. Due to the nature of the quincunx, which makes up a yod, this can indicate a concern with health. Sun quincunx Pluto can also slow down recuperation and can indicate a disturbance in the circulation. The semisextile of the Sun to the Moon can weaken vitality, and the conjunction of the Sun to Mercury adds a nervous component to the health. However, there are indications of a strong constitution and the ability to fight disease. Though posited in the sixth house, Chart F's Sun is within orb of a conjunction to the Descendant, thus gaining strength as an angular Sun. The Sun is also sextile Mars and sextile a Jupiter-Saturn conjunction. This adds to vitality and longevity and is an aid to endurance. The trine of Mars to Jupiter indicates a good blood supply.

Relevant midpoints to the Sun include the Sun 4 Pisces 43 semisquare/sesquiquadrate Mars/Pluto 18 Aries/Libra 14, which could indicate a severe shock such as a heart attack. The Sun is also semisquare/sesquiquadrate Saturn/Neptune 18 Cancer/Capricorn 19, indicating bodily weakness and a propensity to disease. The Sun semisquare/sesquiquadrate Jupiter/Neptune 18 Cancer/Capricorn 39 can indicate a loss of physical power.

The Moon is involved in a fixed T-square and receives no helpful aspects. This can indicate difficult conditions of health and the possibility of a chronic health problem. It is in this fixed T-square that many of the significators of heart disease are represented. An afflicted Moon in fixed signs can indicate an emotional component to disease, most likely emotional repression. The opposition of the Moon to Pluto indicates severe emotional upheaval and the possibility of emotional shock. The Moon's square to the Jupiter-Saturn conjunction is descriptive of a person who alternates between excessive emotionality and complete repression of the emotions, certainly causing tension to the body. Although it would appear that Chart F's Jupiter could lighten

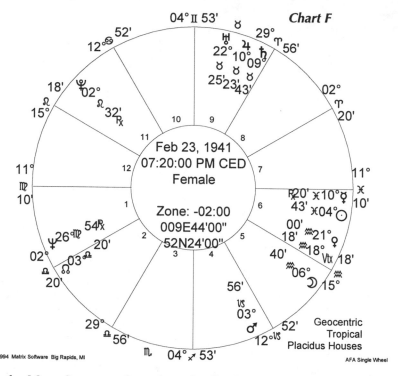

Chart F

04° Ⅱ 53'

Feb 23, 1941
07:20:00 PM CED
Female

Zone: -02:00
009E44'00"
52N24'00"

©1994 Matrix Software Big Rapids, MI

Geocentric
Tropical
Placidus Houses

AFA Single Wheel

up the Moon-Saturn configuration of guilt, depression and insecurity, and Saturn could tone down the emotional gushiness of a Moon-Jupiter square, the opposition of Moon to Pluto describes a person on an emotional roller coaster. The conjunction of the Sun to Mercury in mutable signs and the Moon's tenancy of Aquarius is descriptive of a person prone to stress-related ailments.

Cardiovascular disorders are frequently fixed in nature and involve the fifth and eleventh houses or their rulers. We note the fixed T-square, Saturn, ruler of the fifth house, involved in the T-square and the Moon, ruler of the eleventh house, also afflicted. Problems in the circulation are shown by the afflicted Moon in Aquarius posited in the fifth house opposite Pluto in the eleventh house. The heart muscle and circulatory system are emphasized by the fifth and eleventh house emphasis and also by Venus afflicted in Aquarius in the sixth house. The square of Uranus to Venus disturbs the circulation. The severity of this aspect is further exemplified by Uranus being the most elevated planet in the chart and by Venus being conjunct the Vertex at 18 Aquarius 18 in Aquarius. With Uranus (a malefic) also square the Vertex, this is an indication of a health disorder in fixed signs—all relating to cardiovascular disorders. Note also Venus is semisquare Mars, indicating a disturbance in the equilibrium of the body.

The Moon 6 Aquarius 40 semisquare/sesquiquadrate Saturn/Pluto 21 Gemini/Sagittarius 08 indicates a possible tragedy or great suffering. Chart F was

62

advised by her physician to avoid stressful situations so as not to put undue pressure on her heart.

Chart F's Virgo rising is a good conductor of energy due to its rulership by Mercury. Natal Mercury receives a close sextile from the Jupiter-Saturn conjunction and is strengthened by its conjunction to the Descendant. Again, however, it adds a nervous component to her health and a tendency toward worry. The trine from the Jupiter-Saturn conjunction to the Ascendant would normally give endurance and support to the physical body, but the Jupiter-Saturn conjunction is weakened by a sesquiquadrate from Neptune and a square from the Moon. A hard aspect between Saturn and Neptune can indicate a difficult health problem, and there is a further weakening of the body with Neptune being posited in the first house and square Mars. Mars-Neptune in hard aspect can indicate body toxicity and possible retention of toxins. There is a belief among some medical practitioners that a colonic condition in the body leads to a retention of toxins in the body that can block circulation and cause a heart attack. Chart F's chart, with its fixed T-square strongly affecting the heart and circulation, a Mars-Neptune aspect indicating toxicity and a yod configuration containing the Sun, all point to the possibility of a toxic colon in combination with circulatory disorders. Afflictions to the Sun can indicate a disturbance to Leo, ruler of the heart muscle. Pluto is the natural ruler of the colon and is badly afflicted. It is also quincunx Mars, co-ruler of Scorpio. Although there are no planets in Scorpio, past experience in medical astrology has shown me the validity of using the polarities and/or emphases in a quadruplicity as a possible site of disease. The Jupiter-Saturn conjunction is also a further example of heart disease. This combination is a signature for arteriosclerosis—hardening of the arterial walls. Jupiter, ruler of arterial flow, is impeded by its conjunction to Saturn and its involvement in a fixed T-square.

There are thirteen points in the fixed quadruplicity and fourteen points in the mutable quadruplicity. However, using one point for each planet, six out of ten planets are fixed. The fixed T-square falls in succedent and cadent houses. Mutable disorders are seen by the mutable angles in hard aspect to a mutable Sun. Chart F is known to be very nervous and high strung and has difficulty in handling stress. Her angular Mercury only intensified her susceptibility to illness due to stress. Mercury is also in hard aspect to the angles. The quincunx of Mars to the Midheaven indicates an affliction to an angle, possibly indicating a muscular disorder, fever or a need to control impulsive action. The strongest angular affliction involving heart disease is shown by Uranus square Venus conjunct the Vertex, as described earlier.

In examining some of Chart F's midpoints, Mars is at 3 Capricorn 56 semisquare/sesquiquadrate Sun/Pluto 18 Taurus/Scorpio 38—overexertion, Uranus 22 Taurus 25 square Pluto/Ascendant 21 Leo/Aquarius 51—much anxiety. Uranus is also midpoint Mercury/Pluto 21 Taurus/Scorpio, which can indicate a crisis or nervous breakdown. This can also be shown by Chart F's Ascendant 11 Virgo 10 semisquare/sesquiquadrate Uranus/Neptune 24 Cancer/Capricorn 40.

Chart F's metabolic activity is not consistent. On the one hand, metabolic activity is increased by a sextile of the Sun to Mars and Jupiter. However, it is decreased by the emphasis in fixed and earth signs. The quincunx of Pluto to the Sun alters the metabolism while an angular Sun increases it. There is also a mutable emphasis in the chart which increases metabolic activity and is an aid to throwing off disease.

It would appear that Chart F is prone to heart disease due to a strain on the heart caused by stress. As stated previously, there can be body toxicity and weakness. Chart F has the ability to resist further heart attacks or to regain her health once she comes to terms with her emotional problems. Chart F's main source of emotional stress is caused by a tremendous power struggle with her mother (Moon opposite Pluto posited in the fifth and eleventh houses) and difficulties with her daughter, the fifth house ruling children.

All afflictions involve signatures for heart disease. Chart F's first acute myocardial infarction occurred on May 22, 1975. A solar eclipse at 19 Taurus 59 fell on natal Uranus on May 11, 1975. Note Uranus is the most elevated planet in the chart (also describing nervous tension) and is in a fixed sign ruling the sixth house of health. In April 1975, Chart F's progressed Moon entered Taurus, a fixed sign and a critical degree. On May 25, 1975 a lunar eclipse at 3 Sagittarius 25 fell closely conjunct the IC/Midheaven axis and closely square the Sun. This was a few days after the heart attack and may describe the change in Chart F's life caused by having a heart attack. Transiting Mars was applying by under two degrees to Chart F's True South Node at 2 Aries 01, conjunct her eighth house, triggering a crisis situation. Mars transits usually come early. Transiting Jupiter was in Chart F's eighth house during the attack, thus affording her cosmic protection. Pluto by transit was exactly trine to Chart F's Moon. With natal Pluto in the eleventh house and the Moon in the fifth house ruling the eleventh house, this too was a protective influence, especially since the two planets are in opposition in the natal chart. Transiting Pluto at 6 Libra 40 was also equal Venus/Uranus at 6 Aries/Libra 42, which indicates excitability and a possible disturbance of bodily rhythm. Note natal Venus square Uranus. Neptune by transit and retrograde was square the Ascendant with an orb of twenty-seven minutes. This would lower the vitality of the physical body. Transiting Neptune was also square the solar arc directed Moon at 10 Pisces 45, another indication of lowered vitality and possible emotional difficulty. Emotional tension can be seen by transiting Mars = Moon/Uranus 29 Virgo/Pisces 32 on May 21. Again, Mars transits come early. Solar arc directed Pluto at 6 Virgo 37 quincunx natal Moon again brings in the Moon-Pluto opposition. Transiting Jupiter midpoint Sun/Uranus at 13 Aries/Libra 34 (one minute separating) is a fortunate combination affording protection.

Chart F's second myocardial infarction occurred on March 9, 1983. Transiting Mars was opposing the eclipse point before birth at 8 Libra 11 on March 8, 1983. A New Moon at 23 Aquarius 44 fell on Chart F's Venus in Aquarius in her sixth house on February 12, 1983. On February 27, 1983, the Full Moon at 8 Virgo 12 fell in Chart F's twelfth house close to her Ascendant. Health matters are emphasized through the sign Virgo and the emphasis on the Ascendant, which can represent the physical body. The previous solar eclipse occurred on December 15, 1982 at 23 Sagittarius 04, quincunx natal Uranus and widely square Neptune in the first house. Solar arc directed Uranus at 4

Cancer 13 was separating by seventeen minutes from an opposition to natal Mars, indicating a possible disturbance in the circulation. Transiting Saturn at 3 Scorpio 56 (retrograde) was applying by a one minute square to progressed Mars in Aquarius—2 Aquarius 56—a further indication of a circulatory disturbance. Saturn-Mars is also a threat to the life. Progressed Mars was separating from an opposition to progressed Pluto at 2 Leo 03, involving the Leo Aquarius axis—circulatory or heart problems due to overexertion. To offset the square of transiting Saturn to progressed Mars, transiting Saturn was exactly sextile natal Mars during the second heart attack. This implies endurance and resistance.

The second myocardial infarction was not as severe as the first one. And in both cases there were cosmic influences of a helpful nature to offset planetary difficulties. In both cases the Leo-Aquarius axis was emphasized along with other influences. The suddenness of a heart attack can also be seen by Chart F's elevated Uranus, ruler of body circulation.

Chart G—A Case of Hepatitis

An example of a less serious disease will be shown through Chart G, a case of hepatitis. Chart G, a male, was incapacitated with hepatitis (inflammation of the liver) for approximately six weeks. Symptoms can range from flu-like to failure of the liver. There is an incubation period of from three to six weeks that includes gastro-intestinal symptoms, such as nausea and vomiting, accompanied by a fever. Chart G has a history of gastro-intestinal disorders and migraine headaches.

Chart G contains an angular Capricorn Sun involved in a cardinal T-square with Saturn and the Moon. These are indications of a weakened vitality and the possibility of a chronic health disorder. However, Capricorn Sun has the ability to gain bodily strength with age. This, plus a sextile from Mars, can be a sign of longevity, vitality and the ability to fight disease. The semisquare of Jupiter to the Sun can be protective but can also relate to disease caused by excess. The Sun is also strengthened by being angular and parallel to the Ascendant.

The angular Moon's involvement in a cardinal T-square with Saturn and the Sun is an indication of a need to deal with health problems. The Moon's close square to Saturn combined with its wide trine to Jupiter is descriptive of a person who runs the gamut of emotional repression to emotional excess, perhaps manifesting in stomach disorders (see afflicted Moon in Cancer, ruler of the stomach). However, the trine from Jupiter and Mars to the Moon adds optimism and emotional fulfillment to the nature.

Chart G's Capricorn Ascendant is in a critical degree, indicating possible crises in the life. Being in Capricorn, the vital energies flow more easily throughout the body as Chart G ages. The sextile from Jupiter to the Ascendant adds protection to the body. Mars and Uranus in hard aspect to the Ascendant, besides contributing to an erratic nature, personality quirks and a need for freedom and self-assertion, indicate a highly erratic energy level that would benefit from physical activity. Otherwise, the unused energy can manifest as accidents or quarrels with others. The wide square of Neptune to the Ascendant

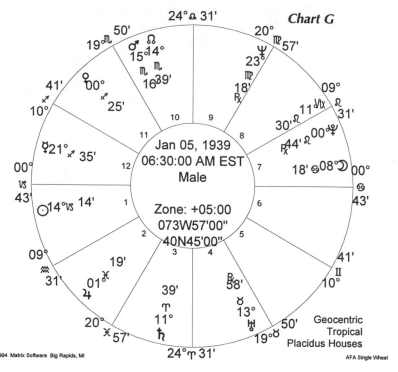

Chart G

24° ♎ 31'

50'
19 ♏

♂ ♓ 0°
15 14°

♏ ♏
16 39'

20°
♍ 57'

♆
23 ℥
♍

18'
℞

09°

41'
♀ 00°
✕

25'
10°
✕

10 9

11 ♍ ♃
30' ♌

♌ 31'
00 ♇
44' ℞ ♌

☿ 21° 35'
✕

12

8

Jan 05, 1939
06:30:00 AM EST
Male

7

18' ⊛ 08° ☽ 00°

00°
♑

43'
☉ 14° ♑ 14'

1

Zone: +05:00
073W57'00"
40N45'00"

6

⊙
43'

09°
♒

31'
01 ✕
♃

19'

2
3   4

5

5

41'
♊
10°

39'

℞
58'
♉
13°

20°
✕ 57'

♈
11°
♄

♅
19 ♉
50'

Geocentric
Tropical
Placidus Houses

©1994 Matrix Software Big Rapids, MI

24° ♈ 31'

AFA Single Wheel

could indicate a propensity to infection.

Chart G's Ascendant 00 Capricorn 42 = Saturn/Neptune 2 Cancer/Capricorn 29. This is an indication of a weakening of the physical body. Pluto's contraparallel to the Ascendant can be descriptive of a difficult change in the body.

Chart G's Saturn 11 Aries 39 = Sun/Moon 11 Aries/Libra 16, which can be descriptive of lowered vitality and chronic health problems, but could also describe an improvement in health as one ages. Chart G's Neptune 23 Virgo 18 = Mars/Pluto 23 Virgo/Pisces 00 may describe his propensity toward an infectious disease such as hepatitis.

Metabolic activity is strengthened by the sextile of Mars to the Sun, the semisquare of Jupiter to the Sun, the trine of Uranus to the Sun and the angularity of Mars, which is also the most elevated planet in the chart. At times the metabolism is hampered by the emphasis of planets in earth and water and the contraparallel of Pluto to the Sun.

A tendency toward excess before his bout with hepatitis may have contributed toward lowering Chart G's immune system. Excessive tendencies are shown by the Sun semisquare Jupiter in the second house, natural house of Taurus. Sun semisquare Venus in Sagittarius can indicate excess and also brings in the sign Sagittarius, one of the rulers of the liver. The Venus in Sagittarius is also square the second house Jupiter, ruler of Sagittarius. Jupiter is further afflicted by a quincunx from Pluto. Pluto is considered a higher octave

66

of Mars and can cause massive infection. Mars is the most elevated planet in the chart. Its position of angularity and elevation makes it stronger than Saturn, thus causing acute infections and inflammation but not necessarily chronic illness.

Mercury in Sagittarius is afflicted by a square from Neptune, thus bringing in more emphasis on Sagittarius and also indicating an affliction in mutable signs. The sign Cancer, which rules the glycogen storage of the liver, is afflicted and angular. There is a cardinal emphasis in the chart, there are afflictions to cardinal angles, all the angles are cardinal, and the Moon, ruler of Cancer, is afflicted in a cardinal T-square. This, combined with the afflictions in mutable signs, in Sagittarius and to Jupiter (ruler of Sagittarius), contributes to the possibility of a health disorder of a gastrointestinal nature, possibly involving the liver, but certainly involving the stomach. Note also Sagittarius on the cusp of the twelfth house, indicating possible confinement. The indications of inflammation, fever and infection are shown by the elevated and afflicted Mars and possibly by Pluto's quincunx to Jupiter.

Chart G has complained not only of gastrointestinal disorders throughout his life, but at one time he thought he had an ulcer. His Mars in Scorpio opposite Uranus could be indicative of a spastic colon. This, plus the quincunx of Mars to Saturn, could describe a need to deal with anger in a healthy manner. Frustration or suppression of anger (and also emotions with Moon square Saturn) can contribute to health problems affecting the gastrointestinal tract or can contribute to his migraine headaches—note Saturn in Aries which also contributes to headaches.

Chart G was incapacitated with hepatitis in February 1982. On December 26, 1981 a lunation fell on his Ascendant, possibly pointing to the incubation period preceding the hepatitis. The last solar eclipse preceding the illness occurred on January 25, 1982 at 4 Aquarius 54, opposite natal Pluto, planet of massive infection.

Transiting Pluto was separating from a conjunction to his Midheaven (angular), indicating severity or a crisis situation and Pluto, massive infection and inflammation. Transiting Neptune was separating from a square to natal Neptune—difficulties with the immune system and the possibility of infection. A Uranus transit separating from a conjunction to natal Venus by two degrees brings in the Sagittarius emphasis. Transiting Saturn (retrograde) conjunct the Midheaven by two and a half degrees may indicate a lowering of vitality or resistance. The emphasis on the Midheaven by Pluto and Saturn indicates the possibility of a disease emphasizing the cardinal quadruplicity, an acute situation with ability for rapid recovery.

On December 24, 1981, transiting Saturn was midpoint Mars/Neptune 19 Aries/Libra 17—the incubation period involving infection. On January 15, 1982, transiting Jupiter was semisquare/sesquiquadrate Mars/Pluto 23 Virgo/Pisces 00, bringing in the rulership of Sagittarius and an axis of excessive (Jupiter) inflammation (Mars/Pluto).

On February 9, 1982 transiting Uranus was semisquare/sesquiquadrate Mars/Neptune 19 Aries/Libra 17. Natal Uranus is angular and Mars/Neptune is an axis ruling body toxicity.

In February 1982, Chart G's progressed Moon at 8 Aquarius 22 was quincunx natal Moon, a health aspect involving an angular planet and the possibility for change.

Progressed Mars at 11 Sagittarius 34 was approaching by trine to natal Saturn, indicating endurance and steady recovery. Saturn is both chart ruler and ruler of Chart G's Sun.

Predictive techniques in this case are more useful in retrospect as there are a number of possibilities of events that could have occurred to Chart G. What can be seen is that there did not appear to be a threat to the life and although hepatitis can become quite serious, in this case recovery was rapid.

Author's Note: Subsequent to the publication of this book, Chart G was diagnosed with a brain tumor that resulted in his death.

Chart H—A Case of Adult-Onset Diabetes Mellitus

Chart H is that of a victim (female) of adult diabetes mellitus, a metabolic disorder. With diabetes mellitus the pancreas does not produce sufficient insulin to burn up carbohydrates. This results in high blood sugar. Symptoms of diabetes include an unusual thirst, throat inflammation, frequent urination, weight loss despite a big appetite, weakness, and itching and boils at times. Diabetics are prone to infection and heal poorly. There can be renal and retinal impairment.

Natal Sun in Gemini is angular and opposite the Ascendant and receives hard aspects from Venus, Jupiter, and Uranus. The combination of the Sun's conjunction to Uranus and the emphasis in mutability indicates an erratic vitality and is descriptive of a person prone to stress and nervous disorders. Jupiter and Venus aspecting the Sun can be an indication of excess and carbohydrate abuse, a possible contributory factor to diabetes. An almost exact parallel of Saturn to the Sun is an indication of a weakened constitution. Sun parallel Pluto can be body transformation.

The Sun 17 Gemini 49 = Mars/Pluto 18 Gemini/Sagittarius 19—chronic disease—semisquare/sesquiquadrate Moon/Neptune 2 Leo 54, indicating a sensitive body. The Sun square Uranus/Ascendant 18 Virgo/Pisces 08—nervousness or a propensity to stress.

Natal Moon in Gemini is not involved in stressful aspects. Its wide conjunction to Mercury indicates a sensitive nervous system. The Moon 2 Gemini 07 semisquare/sesquiquadrate Mars/Neptune 15 Cancer/Capricorn 55 can indicate sensitivity and a propensity to infection.

Sagittarius rising trine Mars indicates a good flow of bodily energies. The square from Jupiter to the Ascendant could be an indication of a propensity to a health disorder relating to excess. Pluto sesquiquadrate the Ascendant can indicate a difficult transformation; Saturn contraparallel the Ascendant puts limits on the body; Uranus contraparallel the Ascendant shows an erratic nature, nervousness and an inconsistency in the flow of vital energies.

The Ascendant 22 Sagittarius 45 semisquare/sesquiquadrate Uranus/Neptune 8 Leo/Aquarius 35 is an indication of hypersensitivity.

The strong emphasis in mutability combined with afflictions to the mutable Ascendant from the Sun, Jupiter, and Pluto and afflictions to the Sun, mutable

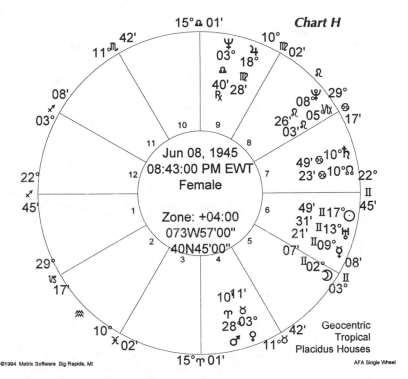

Chart H

Jun 08, 1945
08:43:00 PM EWT
Female

Zone: +04:00
073W57'00"
40N45'00"

Geocentric
Tropical
Placidus Houses

©1994 Matrix Software Big Rapids, MI

AFA Single Wheel

and angular, are all indications of first-degree tendencies to ailments characterized by the mutable quadruplicity, affecting lungs, intestines, nerves or the immune system. Mutable afflictions could point to a health disorder related to the insulin producing pancreas, ruled by Virgo, and also a nervous condition. Natal Pluto is conjunct the Vertex and square Venus in Taurus. Natal Venus is exactly square the Vertex. There is a first degree tendency to a disease of the fixed quadruplicity or the possibility of a chronic disease. The cardinal Midheaven/IC axis is afflicted by hard aspects from the Moon and from Saturn, pointing to a propensity to cardinal related ailments or the possibility of adrenal malfunction or renal impairment.

Metabolic activity is erratic. It is aided by the strong emphasis in mutability—twenty-nine points, the emphasis in air, and Sun parallel Pluto. It is hampered by the Sun parallel Saturn and Sun conjunct Uranus.

An analysis of the possible signatures for diabetes suggest afflictions in Taurus or to Venus to account for an inflamed throat. Natal Venus is afflicted in Taurus by both Mars (conjunct) and Pluto (square), all pointing to throat inflammation. Carter's suggestions of Sun-Uranus and Jupiter-Uranus afflictions for diabetes can be seen by the Sun's conjunction to Uranus and Jupiter square Uranus.

Neptune is the most elevated planet in the chart. This is another indication of a tendency to infection and is also descriptive of the possibility of a coma

(Neptune ruled) that can occur in diabetics. Neptune (which falls in Libra) is also closely quincunx Venus, a health aspect that can affect the sign ruling kidneys and its ruler Venus. And, interestingly enough, afflicted Venus falls in Taurus—sugar consumption.

There is the possibility that diabetes is related to food abuse. A case for disease based on excess can be seen in the Sagittarius rising Ascendant being squared by its ruler Jupiter. Jupiter, in turn, is sesquiquadrate Venus in Taurus. Cancer, ruling the glycogen storage of the liver, is afflicted by the tenancy of Saturn. And ten degrees Cancer, the location of Saturn, is known to be a sign dealing with the pancreas. Saturn at 10 Cancer 49 is midpoint Venus/Jupiter 10 Cancer/Capricorn 50, indicating difficulty in the assimilation of carbohydrates.

Diabetes was diagnosed in February 1982. On January 25, 1982 a solar eclipse at 4 Aquarius 54 fell on F's Antivertex at 5 Aquarius 03, a fixed sign.

Transiting Neptune was separating from a conjunction to the Ascendant (exact during 1981), depleting the flow of vital energies. Transiting Uranus was separating from an opposition to the Moon, indicating a disturbance in bodily rhythm and overstrained nerves. Progressed Moon in Libra was conjunct both progressed and natal Neptune in Libra, again emphasizing the role of the kidneys in elimination of excess sugar from the body, and emphasizing natal Neptune, the most elevated planet in the chart. Jupiter had progressed to a square of the Ascendant, which correlates with the idea of excess.

As can be seen from the foregoing analysis, significators for a metabolic disorder relating to the pancreas are present in the natal chart. Predictive techniques do not indicate a life threatening situation and only in retrospect can their reference to the kidneys, a lowered immune system (Neptune transiting Ascendant) and possible excessive tendencies be seen to correlate with the onset of diabetes.

Chart I—A Case of Phlebitis

Chart I (female) is that of a case of phlebitis, inflammation of a vein, a disease of the circulatory system. Symptoms of phlebitis include tenderness, pain, edema, or a bluish discoloration of the superficial veins. Phlebitis is usually benign, but severe cases can result in lethal pulmonary embolism or chronic venous insufficiency.

Chart I contains the Sun in Aquarius, ruler of circulation, square Aquarius-ruled Uranus. Though not conjunct the Ascendant, the Sun is strengthened by its position in the first house. Uranus square Sun can manifest as erratic vitality, rebellious behavior, and a desire for freedom and excitement. The interception of the Sun in the first house can result in a personality block or difficulties in allowing the personality to manifest, thus causing Aquarius related health problems, i.e., a circulatory disorder.

The Sun is strengthened by a sextile to Mars, which gives vitality and the ability to fight disease. The Sun's contraparallel to Jupiter adds strength to the constitution. Midpoints involving the Sun do not adversely affect I's health.

The Moon, which is involved in a fixed T-square, is aided by a sextile from Neptune. Several hard aspects to the Moon can indicate a concern with health.

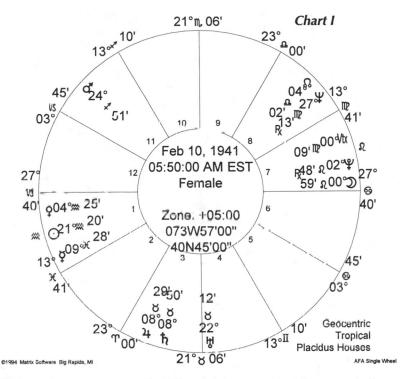

Chart I

21° ♏ 06'

13° ✕ 10'

23° ♎ 00'

45' ♂ ♌ 24°

03° ♈ ✕ 51'

04° ♌ ♎ 13°

02° ♎ ♏ 27° ♆

13° ♏ R

♍ 41'

09' ♍ 00 Ⓥ♈

27° ♍ 40'

♀ 04° ♒ 25'

☊ 21° ♒ 20'

☿ 09° ✕ 28'

48' ♌ 02° ♀

59' ♌ 00° ☽

♌ 27° ♋ 40'

13° ♓ 41'

♋ 45'

♋ 03°

29° 50' 12'

08° 08° ♉ ♉

4 ♄

22° ♉

☿

23° ♈ 00'

10' 13° Ⓟ Ⅱ

21° ♉ 06'

Feb 10, 1941
05:50:00 AM EST
Female

Zone: +05:00
073W57'00"
40N45'00"

Geocentric
Tropical
Placidus Houses

©1994 Matrix Software Big Rapids, MI

AFA Single Wheel

The complex nature of the emotions, as seen in the natal chart, can indicate a psychological basis to health problems. Moon conjunct Pluto is indicative of emotional extremes and can indicate a disease of the blood. I alternates between highs and lows of emotional intensity as she strives for emotional fulfillment— Moon opposite Venus. With the Moon-Pluto conjunction falling conjunct the seventh house cusp of relationships, there can be severe power struggles coupled with a desire for control and the need to learn how to let go The Moon 00 Leo 59 = Mercury/Mars 02 Leo/Aquarius 10 is also an indication of quarreling. This alternates with emotional repression and/or blocks versus an overexpansive nature—Moon opposite an almost exact Jupiter-Saturn conjunction, square an angular Venus in Aquarius with Venus ruling the veins and Aquarius ruling the circulatory system.

The Moon's sextile to Neptune describes an idealistic nature and compassion for others. This, combined with Venus in Aquarius rising and Sun in Aquarius square Uranus suggests the need for an outlet for the rigidity of the fixed T-square and strong emphasis in fixed signs—twenty-two points—possibly working in a helping profession. The Moon 00 Leo 59 opposite Venus/Ascendant 01 Leo/Aquarius 06 also gives the social skills necessary to help others. Circulatory problems could be due to an overly rigid or too conforming nature that does not allow the non-conformity or freedom loving nature of an Aquarius Sun square Uranus to manifest.

The Capricorn Ascendant indicates an improvement of health with age. There can be longevity and endurance. Mars parallel Ascendant is an aid to the flow of bodily energies. The Moon-Pluto conjunction opposite the Ascendant can indicate a fluctuation of the flow of the bodily energies depending on the planetary aspects at any one time.

Chart I exhibits a strong emphasis in the fixed quadruplicity—chronic health disorders that could affect the throat, reproductive system, eliminative organs, the heart and circulatory system. The position of the fixed T-square conjunct the angles is a first degree tendency to a health disorder of the fixed quadruplicity. The emphasis on circulation may be due to the strong Aquarian nature of the chart. Uranus-ruled Aquarius is angular and part of the fixed T-square. Afflictions to the Sun afflict the Leo-Aquarius axis. The Sun is also square the Midheaven, also fixed. An eleventh house Mars is afflicted by Neptune and Uranus. Venus, ruler of venous circulation, is rising and afflicted in Aquarius. It is also quincunx an angular Vertex. A significator of circulatory disorders—Venus, Jupiter, and Saturn in hard aspect—can also be seen in the chart. The afflicted Moon, ruler of fluids, can be an indication of edema.

Venus 4 Aquarius 25 semisquare/sesquiquadrate Moon/Jupiter 19 Gemini/Sagittarius 44 and Moon/Saturn 19 Gemini 54 intensifies the natal T-square involving all four planets with Pluto. Venus semisquare/sesquiquadrate Jupiter/Pluto 20 Gemini/Sagittarius 38, Saturn/Pluto 20 Gemini 49, Mercury/Neptune 18 Gemini/Sagittarius 21, Jupiter/Ascendant 18 Virgo/Pisces 08, and Saturn/Ascendant 18 Pisces 18 are more indications of a possible disturbance in the circulation.

Metabolic activity is strengthened by the sextile of Mars to the Sun and by the tenancy of Mars, the most elevated planet in the chart, in Sagittarius. Metabolic activity is slowed down due to the emphasis in earth signs and the fixed cross, and by the square of Neptune to Mars and the quincunx from Uranus to Mars.

Chart I was stricken with phlebitis on November 23, 1983. Symptoms were a bluish discoloration on the calf of the left leg. The condition involved no blood clots and was not considered serious by her physician. At the time, transiting Pluto was applying by twenty minutes to a square of the natal Moon. This set off the Moon-Pluto conjunction and T-square involving Venus square Jupiter-Saturn, all significators of a circulatory disturbance. Transiting Neptune was separating from a square to natal·Neptune (forty-one minutes), which can be an indication of lowered vitality. Transiting Saturn was separating from an opposition to Jupiter conjunct Saturn—fixed and a significator of a circulatory disorder. Uranus at 8 Aquarius 40, ruler of Aquarius-ruled circulation, was quincunx the Jupiter-Saturn conjunction. The quincunx is an aspect of health and work and is an additional aspect affecting the Jupiter-Saturn conjunction.

Transiting Neptune was separating by three degrees to a conjunction of natal Mars—body weakness and lowered immune response. Transiting Neptune closely semisextile the natal Ascendant is another indication of bodily weakness. Progressed Moon at 05 Pisces 12 on November 23, 1983 was in the twelfth house of the progressed chart and separating from a semisextile to natal

Venus, setting off another significator of circulation. Progressed Venus at 27 Pisces 45 sextile the Ascendant indicated good health and happiness. Despite having phlebitis for two months, Chart I was able to continue a normal life and eventually was completely cured with no reoccurrence.

The natal chart has strong suggestions of the possibility of a circulatory disorder. Again, however, predictive techniques are easier understood in retrospect. The transits to the natal fixed T-square could have resulted in psychological problems, physical problems, or a specific event. The angularity of the fixed T-square being hit by transiting Pluto suggests there would have been a situation of some significance, possibly affecting health. The ability to resist disease, as seen in the natal chart, combined with predictive techniques that were significant but did not to appear to be life threatening, probably contributed to the fact that Chart I's case of phlebitis was not severe.

Chart J—A Case of Myotrophic Lateral Sclerosis (ALS), Lou Gehrig's Disease

Chart J is that of a male diagnosed with amyotrophic lateral sclerosis, a motor neuron disease of unknown cause and no effective cure. The disease results in the progressive degeneration of nerve cells in select areas of the spinal cord. It occurs with greater frequency in males, usually after age fifty-five. Symptoms involve muscle wasting and muscle weakness in the hands, arms, shoulders, and legs. Chewing, swallowing, and talking become difficult as the disease progresses. There can be progressive muscular atrophy leading to a loss of all muscle functions. It generally takes several years before there can be total disability. Before ALS is diagnosed, muscular sclerosis, spinal compression, or a brain tumor must be ruled out.

In examining the chart, one would expect to find an emphasis in planets and signs having to do with locomotion, afflictions involving Mars, which rules the muscles of the body, and afflictions involving Mercury, which rules the nervous system. At first glance, one sees that the natal Sun is in Aquarius, ruling the lower legs, conjunct Mercury, a planet having to do with locomotion, in Aquarius, and that Mars is conjunct the Ascendant in Sagittarius, a sign of locomotion ruling the hips and thighs. As will be seen, Mars and Neptune are in mundane square to each other, a signature corresponding to muscle (Mars) wasting (Neptune).

Sun in Aquarius can be indicative of lumbar disorders and lower leg cramping, swollen legs, spinal disorders, and locomotor disturbances. Aquarius usually denotes a strong constitution with its main complaints being poor circulation and nervous disorders. With Chart J's Sun conjunct Mercury, the nervous system can be weakened and disease can involve the connective tissues. As stated earlier, Mercury in Aquarius also emphasizes ailments having to do with muscles and/or pain in calves or ankles. ALS is a disease of unknown origin, but if poor health habits can weaken the body and contribute to disease, the individual with Sun conjunct Mercury may be overly subjective and not see the part he or she plays in contributing to illness. And an Aquarian Sun tends to neglect diet and skip or forget meals, living on nervous energy.

The nervous component can also be seen with Mercury square Uranus—

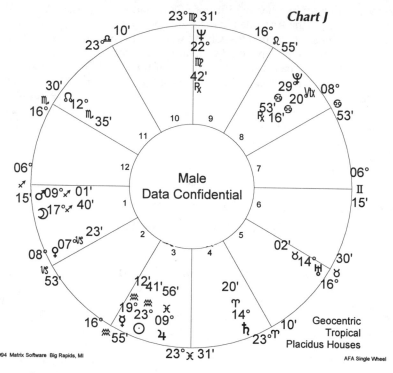

Chart J

23° ♏ 31'

23 ♎ 10'

16° ♌ 55'

♆ 22° ♍ 42' ℞

30'
16° ♏
♌ 12°
♏ 35'

29 ♀ ♋ 20 ⅏ 08°
53' 16° ♋ 53'
℞ ♋

10   9   8

06°
♐
15' ♂ 09° ♐ 01'
☽ 17° ♐ 40'

12   7

Male
Data Confidential

06°
♊
15'

1   6

08° ♀ 07° ♑ 23'
♑ 53'

2   5

02'
♉ 14° ♅ 30'
16° ♉

3   4

12° 41' 56'
19° ♒ ♒ ♓
16° ☿ 23° 09°
♒ 55' ☉ ♃

20'
♈ 14°

♄ 10'
23° ♈

Geocentric
Tropical
Placidus Houses

23° ♓ 31'

©1994 Matrix Software Big Rapids, MI

AFA Single Wheel

nervous haste and a need to rest more. This, combined with Mars in a fire sign rising, can indicate burnout. Propensity to nervous disorders is shown by a mutable emphasis, an afflicted Mercury, a third house emphasis, Neptune in a mutable sign, afflictions to the ruler of the third and ninth houses, Mercury conjunct the Sun, and Mercury quincunx Neptune—weak nerves. Midpoints that support this include Mercury 19 Aquarius 12 semisquare/sesquiquadrate Mars/Pluto 4 Libra 27—chronic nerve disorder brought on by excessive work or stress and Mercury 19 Aquarius 12 semisquare/sesquiquadrate Saturn/Neptune 3 Cancer 31—a nervous disease or debility.

Chart J's Sun semisquare Venus alters the equilibrium and can contribute to disorders resulting from excess. The inconjunct of the Sun to an elevated and angular Neptune indicates an on-again, off-again resistance to disease, inconstant energy, and a tendency to general bodily weakness. H may also be allergic to synthetic fibers, animal fur and various foods.

The Moon in Sagittarius generally gives good vitality and resistance to disease. Negatively, it can indicate weak hips and thighs, locomotor ataxia, and nervous disorders. Its trine to Saturn aids the health and endurance of the body. But the inconjunct to Uranus indicates an erratic energy level and nervous disorders. The Moon's square to Neptune also lowers resistance and can indicate depleted energy, a lack of tone, and excess fluid in the tissues. The Moon's sesquiquadrate to Pluto alters recuperative ability and adds to the one-sidedness of the nature.

The Sagittarius Ascendant being fire adds to the recuperative powers of the body but contributes to locomotor disturbances and nervous disorders. The semisextile of Venus to the Ascendant and Jupiter square the Ascendant both describe overindulgence and/or illness resulting from excess. Mars conjunct (and parallel to) the Ascendant is both a help and a hinderance. It aids the flow of energy throughout the body and gives the ability to bounce back from sickness. Though normally it gives a strong constitution, people with Mars rising can take their health for granted and neglect it. Mars rising can also describe a workaholic (which Chart J admits to being) and overstrained adrenal glands leading to adrenal exhaustion and muscular disorders. This is exacerbated by Mars 09 Sagittarius 01 conjunct Sun/Neptune 8 Sagittarius 12— weakened adrenal gland function. Mars in Sagittarius can also indicate inflammation of the lower cord.

With three planets in the first house, Chart J might be described as a first house type. Like Mars rising, the body can break down due to stress. The individual is always competing to be first, does not get enough rest, and has a poor use of energy.

In examining the quadruplicities by points, there is a mutable emphasis. First degree propensity in the mutable cross is also shown by Neptune conjunct the mutable Midheaven and Mars conjunct the mutable Ascendant. There is a mental and nervous component to mutable cross illnesses as well as a tendency to a clogged lymph gland system. Chart J is weakest in the earth element, indicating a tendency toward poor health habits, thus ignoring the needs of the body. This is reinforced by Neptune conjunct the Midheaven, which can indicate dreaminess and a reluctance to deal with harsh realities. Eating heavy foods such as potatoes and grains would strengthen the earth element and possibly give a grounding to the nature.

Among the significators for a locomotor disorder seen in Chart J's chart are mutability, as previously described, Sagittarius and Gemini on the angles, Mercury and Jupiter in the third house or a third and ninth house emphasis. Mercury and Jupiter are both in the third house with the signs Aquarius on the third house cusp and Leo on the ninth house cusp—both having rulership over the spinal cord. Mars 9 Sagittarius 01 is conjunct Sun/Neptune 8 Sagittarius 12. This is another indication of weak muscular power. Mercury square Uranus can indicate nerve excitability and spastic conditions involving the spinal cord. Mercury inconjunct Neptune can indicate nerve weakness, numbness, and loss of feeling. Mars square Jupiter can indicate irritability of muscle activity. As mentioned earlier, Mars and Neptune are in mundane aspect. *Larousse Encyclopedia of Astrology* describes this as an aspect measured along the celestial equator in right ascension in contrast to a zodiacal aspect which is measured along the ecliptic in celestial longitude. "Since the meridian is by definition at right angles to the horizon, a planet conjunct the Midheaven is in mundane square to a planet conjunct the Ascendant, even though the same two planets may be in zodiacal trine."[35]

This aspect points to the possibility of a wasting disease involving the muscles (Mars) limiting locomotion (Sagittarius), possibly caused by weakened adrenal function (Mars-Neptune) caused by burnout (Mars conjunct the Ascendant) and a weakened auto-immune function (Mars-Neptune). Neptune dissipates the energy of Mars and undermines the body's ability to defend itself.

Chart J was diagnosed with ALS in April 1993. He first began experiencing symptoms in October 1992. At that time solar arc Pluto was applying by five minutes to a conjunction of the Midheaven. The Ascendant by solar arc was applying within five minutes to an opposition to natal Pluto—both at twenty-nine degrees—a critical degree, with natal Pluto in the eighth house, a house of crises. Transiting Pluto was applying to a square to the Sun. Pluto can bring something dormant to light and can affect bodily transformation. Pluto can also indicate toxicity which is another indication that an elimination of toxic buildup in the body by an elimination diet can improve immune function and aid H's recovery.

Saturn by transit was applying to a conjunction of natal Mercury (exact in January 1993) and then natal Sun (exact in March 1993). The progressed Moon at 4 Sagittarius 52 was in the twelfth house, applying by two degrees to the first house—an emphasis on the physical body in the sign of locomotion, Sagittarius. Perhaps its progression through the natal twelfth house was the beginning of an emphasis on the immune system.

Chart J's resistance to disease is helped by an emphasis in fire and air, an angular Mars and the same mutable emphasis described earlier which can describe a disease which disperses itself. Sun in Aquarius can overcome and fight disease. Since a major weakness appears to be the immune system, this area needs to be strengthened. With the mental component of mutability, a positive use the of angular Neptune could be creative and spiritual work of an artistic, mystical, musical or philosophical type.

At this time Chart J's major complaint is a weakness in the throat area, slurred speech, and a weakening in the legs. Of interest is the fixed star Menkar (Saturn qualities) conjunct Uranus in Taurus (the throat), which can indicate throat or larynx problems. Note also Taurus on the sixth house cusp—though usually an aid to endurance and resistance to disease, negatively it can indicate a severe illness. Ailments can affect throat, neck, ears, tonsils, vocal cords. Chart J is optimistic (Moon in Sagittarius) that he will overcome this potentially, devastating disease and expects to be among the ten percent of the population diagnosed with ALS who completely recover.

Chart K—A Liver Transplant

Chart K is that of a female who received a liver transplant after being diagnosed with Hepatitis B. Unlike Chart G presented earlier (A Case of Hepatitis), where bed rest and medication was needed for recovery, this case presented a far more serious picture in that Chart K's liver was so badly damaged by the Hepatitis B virus, that the only cure possible was a liver transplant.

Hepatitis B is also known as Serum Hepatitis. A Case of Hepatitis depicted Hepatitis A or infectious hepatitis which is not as severe as Hepatitis B. Hepatitis B can be spread by sexual contact or contact with infected blood

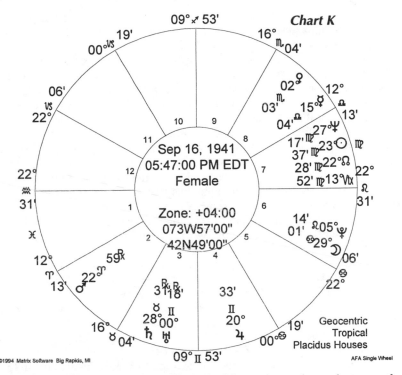

Chart K

09° ♐ 53'

16° ♏ 04'

00° ♑ 19'

06' ♑ 22°

02° ♀
03' ♏
04' ♎   12° ♎
15° ☊   13'
27' ♆

Sep 16, 1941
05:47:00 PM EDT
Female

Zone: +04:00
073W57'00"
42N49'00"

17' ♍ 23 ☉   ♍
37' ♍
28' ♍ 22° ☊   22°
52' ♍ 13 Ⓥ   ♌ 31'

14' ♌ 05° ♇
01'
29' ☽   ♋
06'
22°

22° ♒ 31'

♓

12° ♈
13' ♂ 22° ♉ 59 ℞

3 ℞ ℞
1 18'

♉ ♊
28° 00°
♄ ♅

♊
20°
♃

19' ♋
00° ♋

16° ♉ 04'

09° ♊ 53'

10 9 11 8 12 7 1 6 2 5 3 4

Geocentric
Tropical
Placidus Houses

©1994 Matrix Software Big Rapids, MI

AFA Single Wheel

products. There is an incubation period of from six weeks to three months before the onset of symptoms. Generally, patients with Hepatitis B tend to be more ill, more difficult to treat and take longer to recover than those infected with Hepatitis A. In rare cases there can be total hepatic failure resulting in death. This would have been the case of Chart K, who had only weeks to live without a liver transplant. Chart K had been living in a third world country prior to returning to the United Stated in January 1995. She recalls having dental work done there and feels this may be how she contracted Hepatitis B. Note Chart K's natal Mars at 22 Aries 59 retrograde. The retrograde weakens the action of Mars in Aries which normally would be an aid to fighting infection. Transiting Neptune was square natal Mars on and off during 1994, making its last aspect in January 1995 when Chart K returned to the United States. This combination can be indicative of an infectious disease. The Hepatitis B virus was most likely incubating then. It was late April 1995 that she was diagnosed with Hepatitis B.

In looking for significators of a virus leading to a liver transplant, one would expect to see involvement of the sign Sagittarius and its ruler Jupiter for liver involvement, a hard aspect between Saturn and Jupiter to signify lowered liver function, a signature for infection or lowered immune system (see Chapter Three, Determining Specific Disease States for the significators of lowered immune function), and the involvement of Pluto or Mars and Pluto, both having to do with transplants. As will be seen, these and other significators are all exhibited. One might also wish to see why Chart K was lucky enough to receive a liver transplant and recover. This could be shown by her natal Jupiter trining her Ascendant—protection and good luck.

In the *Encyclopedia of Medical Astrology*, Cornell states that Sun in Virgo afflicted by Jupiter can indicate liver disease. He also includes an afflicted Moon in his description. And he gives the upper lobes of the liver to the sign Cancer and the lower lobes of the liver to Virgo.[36] Chart K does have her Sun in Virgo square Jupiter. And note the Moon in Cancer at twenty-nine degrees, a critical degree, in the sixth house square Mars and conjunct Pluto.

For liver dysfunction, one would also expect to find afflictions involving the mutable cross since Sagittarius is a mutable sign. By a point count, Chart K has an emphasis in the mutable cross. Her Midheaven is in a mutable sign and receives a hard aspect from Mars, thus causing a first-degree affliction in the mutable cross. This not only brings in involvement of the liver, but also of the immune system, with Pisces, ruler of the immune system, also being mutable. Natally, Jupiter is twenty-two and a half degrees from natal Saturn, showing the possibility of chronic liver dysfunction.

Natal Sun at 22 Virgo 37 is conjunct Neptune at 27 Virgo 17, which can indicate weak vitality, lowered resistance, and the possibility of infection. Sun quincunx Mars is descriptive of infection and the semisquare of Pluto to the Sun indicates infection can be massive. Natal Neptune is semisquare/sesquiquadrate Mars/Uranus 11 Taurus/Scorpio 38. The Mars/Uranus midpoint can be indicative of an operation. With Neptune there can be weakness, infection, and danger from poisons or narcotics.

Despite these hard aspects, her Sun sextile Moon aids the vitality, and Sun trine the Saturn-Uranus conjunction gives energy and endurance. And Jupiter in an angular house is an aid to longevity.

Chart K's Moon 29 Cancer 01 is conjunct Saturn/Neptune 27 Cancer/Capricorn 54. This is a difficult midpoint relating to the possibility of a chronic condition at that point in the zodiac. Her Moon is also semisquare/sesquiquadrate Mars/Pluto 14 Gemini/Sagittarius 06, indicating the possibility of a drastic change. During the liver transplant, her gallbladder, which is ruled by the sign Cancer, was removed. The gallbladder stores bile produced by the liver but is not necessary for survival.

Chart K's twenty-nine degree Cancer Moon in the sixth house is square Mars at 22 Aries 59 retrograde, describing a possible stomach disorder and conjunct Pluto at 5 Leo 04, an aspect of transformation which can indicate altered bodily rhythms. Moon conjunct Pluto could also describe the drastic change in her domestic life that would occur after the liver transplant—monthly visits to the hospital, dietary changes, inability to work, and medication.

Her Aquarius Ascendant at 22 Aquarius 31 is a good conductor of energy but receives a square from Saturn at 28 Taurus 31, which could describe a chronic health problem. However, the sextile from Mars and trine from Jupiter are an aid to the health and longevity of the physical body.

The Vertex at 13 Virgo 12, an angle having to do with fate, is semisquare/sesquiquadrate Saturn/Neptune and square Mars/Pluto. Again, the possibility is seen for chronic illness, bodily weakness, and the destruction of cells.

This is also a further indication of an afflicted angle (Vertex in Virgo) activating the mutable cross—in this case the immune system (Pisces) and the removal (Mars/Pluto) of the liver ruled by Sagittarius in the mutable cross.

Chart K was diagnosed with Hepatitis B in late April 1995. From that point and well past the date of the liver transplant (May 22, 1995), her life was in danger. One would expect to see predictive aspects both of danger and protection. On April 16 the lunar eclipse at 25 Libra 04 was square her Moon and her Mars. The solar eclipse on April 29, 1995 at 8 Taurus 56 was square natal Pluto. On April 19, Saturn by transit was sesquiquadrate natal Pluto and sesquiquadrate progressed Pluto on April 29. On April 22 and April 27, Saturn by transit was square natal Jupiter—Saturn-Jupiter combinations are the classic signature for liver dysfunction and also rule gallbladder problems. On April 26, transiting Saturn was opposite the progressed Nodes and opposite the natal Nodes on May 13. Saturn Nodes can indicate a hospital stay.

The operation for the liver transplant was May 22, 1995. On May 29, 1995, natal Saturn was opposite the Sun, indicating the lowered vitality and restriction. On June 5, transiting Pluto was opposite Uranus; on June 16, Pluto was opposite natal Saturn; and on June 18, Neptune was semisquare the Midheaven. It is also interesting to note that Chart K had five progressed planets retrograde at this time in her life.

A most interesting combination is seen the day of the liver transplant. The Midheaven/IC had progressed to 29 Cancer/Capricorn 01. Note natal Moon at 29 Cancer 01. This critical degree is now activated and shows the end of a way of life (twenty-nine degrees) and the beginning of a new life to come (zero degrees) as Chart K has to deal with the lifestyle changes necessitated by a liver transplant.

If one uses a ninety degree tri-dial wheel (found in most astrological computer programs) or draws the outer wheels by hand around a ninety degree dial for the day of the transplant with the inner wheel natal, the middle wheel progressions and the third or outer wheel transits for that day, and puts the pointer on natal Saturn, one notes progressed Uranus, and transiting Mars-Pluto equal to natal Saturn (on the dial) with the aforementioned natal Pluto at twenty-two and a half degrees on one side of Saturn and natal Jupiter at twenty-two and a half degrees on the other side of Saturn. These are all planetary pictures dealing with a possible liver dysfunction, a transplant, an operation, and a life in danger—all obviously interpreted after the fact.

On May 19, prior to the operation, the progressed Moon was trine the progressed Sun. On May 26, transiting Uranus was trine natal Uranus and on May 27, transiting Pluto was trine the natal Moon. On June 6, 1995 Jupiter by transit entered Chart K's tenth house. This, along with the positive transits and progressions preceding it, would appear to have been a protective influence. On June 29, Pluto by solar arc was trine natal Saturn, an aid to endurance. Happily, by July 1995, Chart K had returned home from the hospital and was beginning to feel like her old self.

Chapter Five

Homeopathy

A s an alternative to traditional medicine, many persons are turning to
homeopathy and seeking the advice of a homeopathic physician. Modern
homeopathic medicine is based on the work of the German physician Hahne-
mann (1755-1843). Its use spread throughout Europe and continues today.
Homeopathy was in vogue in the 1800s in the United States, but fell out of
favor with the rise of the drug industry after the Civil War, the introduction of
miracle drugs, and other changes in modern medicine.

A homeopathic physician is a medical doctor who has taken a postgraduate
course in homeopathy and a preceptorship with a practicing homeopathic
physician. State Panos and Heimlich in *Homeopathic Medicine at Home*,
"Clinical evidence accumulated over more than 150 years of use demonstrates
that homeopathic medicine is the viable alternative to standard medicine."[37]
In contrast to commonly practiced medicine in the United States—allopathic,
curing disease by administering chemical substances such as drugs, which
suppress symptoms, or through surgery—homeopathic practitioners follow the
law of similars. This can be described as "like cures like," a premise that goes
back to Paracelsus. Instead of trying to suppress a fever, for example, with a
fever suppressant, which is considered an opposite, a homeopathic physician
would prescribe a homeopathic remedy that produces a similar condition—in
this case, a fever—without seriously aggravating it. "Symptoms are recog-
nized as behavioral expressions of disharmony, an indication that the body is
fighting against illness or infection, and are seen as aspects of a whole pattern
which includes all dispositions to health. Symptoms are valuable information
and are therefore to be encouraged in their expression rather than suppressed...The production of such symptoms is accepted as an indication of a
healthy organism seeking to restore balanc,"[38] states A.T. Mann in *Astrology
and the Art of Healing*.

A homeopathic remedy consists of substances that in larger quantities
would cause the particular symptom. The homeopathic physician believes that
the use of opposites suppresses the body's natural healing abilities and opposes
and delays the healing process. It is believed that using a similar remedy

supports the body's natural healing ability without making the condition worse.

These conclusions are based on what is termed "proving." Under scientifically controlled conditions, healthy subjects were given a daily dose of a homeopathic substance and the symptoms recorded. These symptoms became part of a remedy picture that are listed in the *Materia Medica*, the homeopathic physician's primary reference.

In allopathic medicine, the doctor usually tries to give a name to the symptoms exhibited by a patient. A homeopathic physician considers the whole person. His aim is to strengthen the body to resist germs. The homeopathic physician needs to know the entire medical and psychological history of the patient. The patient is then treated according to both his personality and the nature of his or her symptoms, such as what time of day they occur and any corresponding ailments that occur with the symptoms. Even such particulars as food tastes are taken into consideration. The homeopathic physician then prescribes a remedy that reflects the entire range of symptoms. Since there are thousands of remedies available, except for first-aid use by the layman, only a licensed homeopathic physician should prescribe a treatment. "The cure is the activation and removal of the symptoms in the reverse sequence in which they appeared from the physical, emotional, and mental bodies."[39]

Homeopathic remedies offer a viable alternative for those who are afraid of the side effects of modern drugs. Homeopathic substances are made of materials obtained from animal, vegetable, and mineral sources. They are non-toxic and do not cause side effects, and they are much cheaper to purchase than prescription and non-prescription drugs. Homeopathic remedies are considerably diluted so as to produce a mild stimulation and not a violent reaction, as some allopathic medicine can produce. Large doses are considered detrimental while small doses are considered stimulating. Homeopathic remedies are prepared by successively diluting and shaking or pulverizing the remedy with milk sugar until minute amounts of the original substance remain. These small doses are called potencies or alterations. They can be likened to trace minerals which are needed in only minute amounts by the body. The potentized remedy cannot act directly on tissues so is considered non-toxic and will not cause side-effects. A homeopathic physician, in most cases, will only prescribe one remedy at a time. Using remedies in combination is not as well documented. (For a discussion of homeopathic remedies in combination based on planetary aspects, see the author's note at the end of the chapter). Though success stories of homeopathy abound in the literature, there is no known theory as to why and how homeopathy works. Much like astrology, it works despite the inability to substantiate it directly. It has been mentioned in the literature that homeopathy has an etheric quality about it.

Homeopathy is used in both acute and chronic cases of illness. States Dr. William Gutman, M.D., in *The Little Homeopathic Physician*, "Homeopathy, the same as any other method of treatment, is limited only to those cases where nature can no longer produce a reaction."[40]

For those wishing to use homeopathic remedies as a first-aid measure, the 6x potency in tablet form would be the most useful. In an acute situation, one would take two tablets every two to four hours. Remedies should be taken in a clean mouth and allowed to dissolve beneath the tongue. Homeopathic remedies also come in granules and tinctures. Granules can be used if a patient is unconscious. A tincture is a solution of alcohol which is usually mixed with a lotion and used externally. If there is no effect from the remedy, it is possible the wrong remedy was used.

A useful book for an introduction to the benefits of homeopathy is *Homeopathic Medicine at Home* by Panos and Heimlich. Since homeopathy is both an art and a science and involves a lifetime of study, serious illness should be treated by a professional to avoid possible harm.

Following is a list of some homeopathic remedies useful for first-aid. It would take an entire book to list all the possible remedies, even for the layman. For example, there are several remedies for a cold and/or cough depending on the symptoms one is exhibiting. The following list summarizes some useful remedies. For best results one should correlate the description of symptoms listed in the *Materia Medica* with a particular remedy along with the symptoms one is exhibiting.

Aconitum: Useful at the onset of a fever. A dose every half hour to an hour until perspiration sets in. Remedy for tension headaches, inability to tolerate bright light.

Ammonium Bromatum: Coughs.

Antimonium Crudum: Overeating.

Arnica: Considered the most useful remedy to have on hand, useful for injuries of every description, especially sore muscles and bruises. Shock. Helpful also for the venous system.

Arsenicum Album: Food poisoning, diarrhea, vomiting.

Belladonna: An alternative to those allergic to penicillin for treatment of strep throat; remedy for acute fevers, cramps.

Byronia: An alternative to phenobarbital for colic, remedy for slowly developing fever and inflammation.

Calendula officinals: Wounds.

Camphora: Head colds.

Causticum: Weak bladder.

Chamomilla: Nerve remedy.

Colchicum: Morning sickness.

Colocynthis: Colic, cramps.

Gelsemium: As an alternative to aspirin, which can cause gastrointestinal bleeding in susceptible individuals, for tension headache, influenza.

Hypericum Perforatum: Nerve injury.

Ipecacuanha: Nausea.

Ledum: Puncture wounds, insect bites.

Nux Vom: An alternative to habit-forming laxatives, aids digestive system, relief of hemorrhoids.

Ruta Graveolons: Sprains, bruises of bones, corns.

Rhus Toxicodendron: Overexertion, muscle pain, sprains.

Sulphur: Skin conditions such as eruptions.

Symphytum Officinelle: Bone injury.

Tabacum: Seasickness.

Tartarus Meticue: Accumulation of phlegm
Urtica Urens: Burns or scalds
Veratrum Album: Weakness and fainting

Author's Note: Though beyond the scope of this book, those interested may wish to study Wolfgang Dobereiner's Munich Rhythm Theorie. The first volume in the series is entitled Patterns of Experience in the Astrological Diagnosis and Homeopathic Treatment of Illnesses. *In it he states: "...the homeopathic remedies are primarily effective on the level of individual destiny, and only as a result of this do they produce mental and physical effects. For this reason, the astrological remedy pictures describe paths of experience and not a series of peculiar symptoms...the repression of all that is painful and the resistance to certain necessary personal experiences leads then to illnesses which are of a higher order, illnesses which touch the individual's destiny...From the astrological point of view, the prescription of a single homeopathic remedy is, as a rule, insupportable."[41] He feels that when combining remedies, with the exception of Ferrum Phos, one should not simultaneously take dosages from two heavy metals or from two animals of the same type. The potencies of the remedies must be taken into account so that one remedy does not get in the way of another remedy.*

Chapter Six

Cell Salts

C ell salt therapy, also known as the biochemic system of medicine, is based on treating the individual cells of the body with cell salts (also called mineral salts) until the natural chemical balance of the body has been restored. These inorganic chemical materials are necessary to the proper functioning of the body.

Cell salt therapy was used in Europe as early as the 1800s. It is based on the cell theory of Virchow (1858) and elaborated on by other homeopaths, most notably, Dr. William H. Schuessler of Oldenburg, Germany, a homeopathic physician. Cell salts are used by the body to replenish enzymes in each of the cells. It is felt by practitioners of their use that a deficiency in one of the cell salts—which number twelve—can lead to disease. By administering a small quantity of the deficient cell salt, one should be able to reestablish the correct salt balance in the cell.

Schuessler believed that a deficiency in one of the organic cell salts could result in symptoms that could eventually lead to disease. By studying the symptom of a patient, Schuessler was able to prescribe the correct cell salt until the symptom was relieved and the body restored to health.

Cell salts normally come in the form of tiny tablets which are placed beneath the base of the tongue so as to be absorbed directly into the bloodstream. They can be purchased at a homeopathic pharmacy or health food store. They come in various triturations, a measurement of the fineness of the sieve the salt is put through. The higher the number, the finer the sieve. They are usually found in the six times or twelve times variety, twelve being twice as pulverized as six.

In *Modern Medical Astrology*, Robert C. Jansky, discusses Dr. C.W. Carey who discovered a relationship between the cells' requirements for raw materials and the time of the year. Dr. Carey discovered that the twelve basic cells salts required by the human body seemed to be symbolically related to the twelve signs of the zodiac.[42] The theory is that the body requires larger amounts of the cell salt that corresponds with the sign opposite the natal Sun, the sign occupied by Saturn, the sign occupied by the South Node of the Moon, and the rising sign of the chart. In the case of disease, a homeopathic physician would prescribe the cell salt associated with the Sun sign and its opposite sign and the cell salt symbolic of the disease. The above rules are not foolproof but are only guides as to correct dosage. And persons who are drug sensitive, usually shown by an angular or elevated Moon or Neptune or Neptune in the sixth house, would only require half the dosage.

Following is a list of the twelve cell salts and the zodiac signs that correspond with their use:

Aries
Biochemic Salt: Potassium Phosphate (Kali Phosphate)
Utilization: a nerve nutrient used for mental conditions and disorders, depression, insomnia, hysteria, headache, respiratory problems, irritating skin conditions, lack of pep.

Taurus
Biochemic Salt: Sodium Sulfate (Natrium Sulphuretum)
Utilization: regulates density of intercellular fluids, useful in digestive process, edema, gallbladder conditions, liver ailments, influenza.

Gemini
Biochemic Salt: Kali Muriaticum (Potassium Chloride)
Utilization: A remedy for sluggish conditions, helps regulate the fibrin in the blood, aids skin rashes, respiratory conditions, digestion, burns. In combination with Ferrunm Phos. for inflammation or irritation.

Cancer
Biochemic Salt: Calcium Flouride (Calcareum Fluoricum)
Utilization: Gives tissues quality of elasticity, preserves tooth enamel, fingernails, bone, the lens of the eyes. Used with silica to toughen up body tissue and restore muscle tone.

Leo
Biochemic Sale: Magnesium Phophate (Magnesium Phospharaicum)
Utilization: An anti-spasmodic tissue salt which supplements the action of kali phos. To relieve cramping, muscle spasm, headache, neuralgia, earache, spasmodic twitching, convulsion, hiccups, stomach cramps, flatulence.

Virgo
Biochemic Salt: Potassium Sulfate (Kali Sulpphuricum)
Utilization: concerned with the manufacture and distribution of the body's oily secretions in the skin and the hair, is an important constituent of hair and scalp, and a body lubricant. Aids respiration. Works with Ferr. Phos as an oxygen carrier.

Libra
Biochemic Salt: Natarium Phosphataicum (Sodium Phosphate)
Utilization: an acid neutralizer, used to preserve acid-alkaline balance of the body. May be used to treat gout, rheumatism, insomnia, kidney stones, tired muscles, and ulcers.

Scorpio
Biochemic Salt: Calcium Sulfate (Calcareum Sulphuricum)

Utilization: A blood purifier and healer and disinfectant, a constituent of connective tissue and bone, aids digestion, may alleviate constipation, sore throat, a cold, any toxemia. Helps eliminate organic matter no longer required by the body.

Sagittarius
Biochemic Salt: Silicon Dioxide (Silica)

Utilization: a cleanser and eliminator, restores activity of skin, useful for excess perspiration, pus formation, brittle fingernails. Promotes suppuration and causes discharge of poisonous matter, helps maintain body warmth.

Capricorn
Biochemic Salt: Calcium Phosphate

Utilization: formation of healthy bone tissue, concerned with nutrition, constituent of the digestive juices, aids growth. An aid for anemia, after convalesence. A good tonic.

Aquarius
Biochemic Salt: Natrium Muriaticum (Sodium Chloride)

Utilization: A water distributing tissue salt, useful for blisters, watery swelling, itching, eczema, depression, toothache. Puts moisture back in tissues, production of hydrochloric acid.

Pisces
Biochemic Salt: Iron Phosphate or Ferrum Phos

Utilization: oxygen carrier, used as a supplementary remedy with other cell salts, children's ailments, muscular strain, anemia. Builds blood vessels, nourishes muscles, useful for sore throats, coughs and colds, feverish conditions.

Davidson's Medical Astrology recommends Ferrum Phos for any "itis," an inflammation.[43]

Conclusion

This book was written in order to introduce the reader to the complex subject of medical astrology. The steps outlined in the book are intended as a guide toward giving a health reading. Other medical astrology books were cited as aids in assessing health, for use in researching various disease states, and as sources of various astrological techniques that are helpful in medical astrology.

It behooves anyone who is serious about becoming a medical astrologer to study and utilize as many medical astrology books as possible. It is also recommended that unless the reader is a trained health or medical professional, he or she should also purchase a good medical dictionary and as simplified a text as possible on anatomy. One should also be prepared to spend many hours in a medical library reading journals and/or medical texts in order to better understand a particular disease state. It is one thing to be proficient as an astrologer; it is quite another matter to be able to interpret a chart in terms of health when one has had no training or has not studied this area.

Most beginning astrologers start by interpreting their own chart. This is also good advice for the beginning medical astrologer. If you are aware of a particular health problem, look for the astrological significators. Determine the seriousness of the problem by checking malefics affecting angles. Learn the predictive methods by looking back on times of illnesses or a health crisis. What was happening in your chart at that time? And be careful of falling into the trap that occurs to most beginning astrologers (usually when learning prediction)—assuming the worst of some planetary combination in your chart, not because it shows up in your chart but because you lack the experience to interpret a chart intelligently. Then, when you become proficient in assessing health in your own chart, begin by studying the cases of persons who contracted diseases and again look for the astrological significators. After this much study you should then be ready to interpret for clients, always remembering that in a general health reading the duty of a medical astrologer is to tell the client his or her strengths and weaknesses, as seen in the natal chart, as a preventative measure against future health disorders.

Footnotes

[1]Harry F. Darling, M.D., *Essentials of Medical Astrology* (Tempe, Arizona: American Federation of Astrologers, Inc., 1981), p.6.

[2]Henrich Daath, *Medical Astrology* (Reprinted in Mokelumne Hill, California: Health Research, 1968), p.11.

[3]Ibid, pp.38-39.

[4]Roger Hutcheon, *Planetary Pictures in Declination* (Cambridge, Mass.: A.T.S. Press, 1976) p. 5.

[5]Doris Chase Doane, *Astrology: 30 Years Research* (Tempe, Arizona: American Federation of Astrologers, Inc., 1979), p.41.

[6]Dr. William M. Davidson, *Davidson's Medical Astrology—A Series of Eight Special Lectures on Medical Astrology and Health* (Monroe, New York: Astrological Bureau, 1959), p.5.

[7]W. Davidson, p. 13.

[8]H. Darling, p.28.

[9]Marcia Starck, *Astrology Key to Holistic Health* (Birmingham, Michigan: Seek-It Publications, 1982), p. 74.

[10]Max Heindel and Augusta Foss Heindel, *Astro-Diagnosis A Guide to Healing* (Oceanside, California: The Rosicrucian Fellowship, 1929), p. 183.

[11]W. Davidson, p. 52.

[12]Ronald Harvey, *Mind and Body in Astrology, Guidelines for A New Assessment of Astrology in Medicine* (Romford, Essex, England: L.N. Fowler & Co. Ltd., 1983), pp. 186-187.

[13]Robert Pelletier, *Planets in Aspect* (Gloucester, Massachusetts: Para Research, 1984), p. 228.

[14]R. Harvey, p. 187.

[15]H.L. Cornell, M.D., *Encyclopaedia of Medical Astrology Third Revised Edition* (New York, New York: Samuel Weiser, Inc., 1972), p. 473.

[16]C.E.O. Carter, B.A., *An Encyclopaedia of Psychological Astrology* (London, England: The Theosophical Publshing House, Ltd., 1963), p. 134.

[17]Ibid, p. 37.

[18]Ibid, p. 92.

[19]Ibid, p. 74.

[20]D. Doane, p. 148.

[21]C. Carter, p. 69.

[22]LD. Doane, p. 148.

[23]J. Merrill Harmon, *Complete Astro-Medical Index* (Van Nuys, California: Astro-Analytics Publications, 1975), p. 93.

[24]C. Carter, p. 32.

[25] J. Harmon, p. 93

[26] D. Doane, p. 140.

[27] J. Harmon, p. 90.

[28] W. Davidson, p. 18.

[29] Ibid, p. 74.

[30] Reinhold Ebertin, *The Combination of Stellar Influences* (Tempe, Arizona: American Federation of Astrologers, Inc.), p. 189.

[31] Ibid, p. 138.

[32] Robert E. Rothenberg, M.D., F.A.C.S., *Medical Dictionary and Health Manual Fourth Revised Edition* (New York, New York: New American Library, 1982), p. 111.

[33] R.C. Davison, *The Technique of Prediction* (London, England: L.N. Fowler & Co. Ltd., 1982), p. 65.

[34] R. Ebertin, p. 157

[35] Brau, Jean-Louis Brau, Helen Weaver, and Allan Edmonds: *Larousse Encyclopedia of Astrology* (New American Library, New York and Scarborough, Ontario, 1977), p. 123.

[36] H.L. Cornell, p. 461.

[37] Macsimund B. Panos, M.D. and Jane Heimlic: *Homeopathic Medicine at Home* (G.P. Putnam's Sons, New York, New York, 1980), p. 8.

[38] A.T. Mann: *Astrology and the Art of Healing* (Unwin Paperbacks, London, Englnad, 1989), p. 82.

[39] Ibid, p. 148.

[40] William Gutman, M.D., *The Little Homeopathic Physician* (Philadelphia, Boericke & Tapel, 1961), p. 3.

[41] Wolfgang Dobereiner, *Patterns of Experience in the Astrological Diagnosis and Homeoapthic Treatment of Illnesses* (Munich Rhythm Theory Press, Munich, Germany, 1983), p. 259.

[42] Jansky, Robert C.: *Modern Medical Astrology* (Astro-Analytics Publications, Van Nuys, Califronia, 1978), p. 16.

[43] W. Davidson, p. 118.

[44] To obtain midpoints in round numbers quickly, T. Patrick Davis' *Midpoint Calculator* is very easy to use and inexpensive - $2.00 plus postage and handling from the American Federation of Astrologers).

[45] An easy to read format of midpoint structures is available as an option from Astro Computing Scrices, 1-800-888-9983.

Glossary

Adrenal Medulla: The central portion of the adrenal gland, responsible for production and secretion of adrenaline.

Anatomy: The science of structure of the body or its organs

Aorta: The large artery originating from the left ventricle of the heart.

Arrhythmia: Lack of rhythm, applied especially to irregularities of heart beat.

Benign: Not cancerous; not malignant.

Capillaries: Very small blood vessels.

Cardiomyopathy: Disease of the heart muscle.

Catarrh: Irritation of a membrane, particularly of the respiratory tract, accompanied by an excessive secretion of mucus.

Collagen Diseases: Those associated with disturbances in the connective tissues, such as that around joints, arteries, etc.

Dermatitis: Inflammation of the skin.

Diabetes Mellitus: A chronic disease characterized by inability to burn up the sugars and starches (carbohydrates) which have been ingested. It is caused by insufficient production of insulin by the pancreas.

Duodenitis: Inflammation of the duodenum; a common condition often associated with excess excretion of acid by the stomach.

Duodenum: The first portion of the small intestine, commencing immediately after the stomach.

Dysmenorrhea: Painful or difficult menstruation.

Embolism: The obstruction of an artery by an embolus, usually a piece of clotted blood which breaks away from one part of the circulatory system and travels to another.

Embolus: Something breaking off from one part of the body and traveling through the blood stream to another.

Endocarditis: Inflammation of the valves or lining membrane of the heart.

Endocardium: The membrane lining the chambers of the heart.

Femur: The thigh bone, originating in the hip and extending down to the knee.

Fibrocystic Disease: Tissue which has become cystic and fibrous.

Fistula: An abnormal canal or tract, often occurring in or about the anus.

Functional Disorder: A disorder caused by an upset in function rather than an actual disease.

Hepatic: Referring to the liver.

Ilium: The expansive superior portion of the hip bone.

Insulin: A hormone produced in the cells of the pancreas for the metabolism and utilization of sugar.

Ischium: The bone upon which one places his weight when sitting.

Islets of Langerhans: The cells in the pancreas which secrete insulin.

Jaundice: Yellow discoloration of the skin and eyes due to bile pigments in the blood.

Lumbago: Lower back pain.

Lympathic System: The vessels or channels which carry lymph.

Lymphoma: A tumor composed of lymph node tissue.

Meninges: The thin membranes covering the brain and spinal cord.

Metastasis: The travel of disease from one organ or part to another not directly connected with it.

Myocarditis: Inflammation of the heart muscle.

Myocardium: Heart muscle.

Nephritis: Inflammation of the kidneys.

Neuralgia: Pain along the route of a nerve.

Node: A small mass of tissue in the form of a swelling or protuberance which is either normal or pathological.

Organ: A specialized body structure which performs a specific function (the ear is the organ of hearing, the intestine is the organ of digestion).

Organic Disease: Disease associated with changes in the structure of an organ.

Pancreas: A large gland, six to eight inches long, lying crosswise posterior in the upper portion of the abdomen. It secretes enzymes into the intestines for the digestion of food and it manufacturers insulin which it secretes into the bloodstream.

Pericarditis: Inflammation of the sheath surrounding the heart.

Pericardium: The sheath of tissue encasing the heart.

Peritonitis: Infection of the abdominal lining (peritoneum) following the rupture of an appendix or other intestinal organ.

Pharynx: The area in back of the nose and mouth; the throat.

Physiology: The science dealing with the study of the functions of tissues or organs.

Pituitary Gland: An important endocrine gland located at the base of the brain.

Pleura: The membrane lining the chest cavity and covering the lungs.

Pulmonary: Pertaining to the lungs.

Renal: Pertaining to the kidneys.

Retina: The innermost layer of the eye, the sensitive organ upon which light rays are focused.

Saphenous Veins: The large system of veins in the legs and thighs which drain the superficial tissues of the lower limbs.

Sternum: The breastbone in the front of the chest.

Tissue: An aggregation of cells which are similar in type, such as fat tissue, brain tissue, connective tissue, etc.

Toxemia: A condition caused by poisonous products in the blood with resultant illness.

Trachea: The windpipe.

Ureter: The tube leading from the kidney to the bladder.

Urethra: The tube leading from the urinary bladder to the outside.

Vas Deferens: The tube carrying sperm from the testicles to the glands where they are stored in preparation for ejaculation.

Vasomotor Mechanism: That which regulates the contraction or dilatation of blood vessels.

General Bibliography

1. Arroyo, Stephen: *Astrology, Psychology, And The Four Elements*, CRCS Publications, Davis, California, 1975.

2. *Atlas Of Human Anatomy* (Revised) Text by Samuel Smith, Barnes & Noble Books, New York, 1961.

3. Berkow, Robert, Editor-in-Chief: *The Merck Manual Of Diagnosis & Therapy, Volume 1 General Medicine Fourteenth Edition*, Merck Sharp & Dohme Research Laboratories, Rahway, NJ, 1982.

4. Berkow, Robert, Editor-in-Chief: *The Merck Manual Of Diagnosis & Therapy, Volume II Obstetrics, Gynecology, Pediatrics, Genetics*, Merck Sharp & Dohme Research Laboratories, Rahway, NJ, 1982.

5. Bills, Rex E.: *The Rulership Book*, Macoy Publishing & Masonic Supply Co., Inc., Richmond, Virginia, 1976.

6. Brau, Jean-Louis, Weaver, Helen and Edmands, Allan: *Larousse Encyclopedia Of Astrology*, New American Library, New York and Scarborough, Ontario, 1977.

7. Bland, Jeffrey: *Nutraorobics*, Harper & Row, San Francisco, California, 1985.

8. Carter, C.E.O.: *An Encyclopaedia Of Psychological Astrology*, The Theosophical Publishing House Ltd., London, England, 1963.

9. Chapman, J.B., M.D. and Perry, Eduard L., M.D.: *The Biochemic Handbook*, Formur, Inc., St. Louis, Missouri, 1976.

10. Cornell, H.L.: *Encyclopaedia Of Medical Astrology*, Samuel Weiser, Inc., York Beach, Maine, 1972.

11. Daath, Heinrich: *Medical Astrology*, Health Research, Mokelumne Hill, California, 1968.

12. Darling, Harry F.: *Essentials Of Medical Astrology*, American Federation of Astrologers, Inc., Tempe, Arizona, 1981.

13. Davidson, William: *Davidson's Medical Astrology*, Astrological Bureau, Monroe, New York, 1979.

14. David, Adelle: *Let's Get Well*, Harcourt Brace Jovanovich, Inc., New York, New York, 1972.

15. Davison, R.C.: *The Technique Of Prediction*, L.N. Fowler & Co. Ltd., London, England, 1972.

16. Doane, Doris Chase: *Astrology 30 Years Research*, American Federation of Astrologers, Inc., Tempe, Arizona, 1979.

17. Dobereiner, Wolfgang: *Patterns Of Experience In The Astrological Diagnosis And Homeopathic Treatment Of Illnesses*, Munich Rhythm Theory Press, Munich, Germany, 1983.

18. Ebertin, Reinhold: *Astrological Healilng The History And Practice Of Astromedicine*, Samuel Weiser, Inc., York Beach, Maine, 1989

19. Ebertin, Reinhold: *Applied Cosmobiology*, Ebertin-Verlag, 7080 Aalen, Germany, 1972.

20. Ebertin, Reinhold: *The Combination Of Stellar Influences*, American Federation of Astrologers, Inc., Tempe, Arizona.

21. Greaves, Doris E.: *Cosmobiology: A Modern Approach To Astrology*, The American Federation of Astrologers, Tempe, Arizona, 1980.

22. Gutman,M.D., William: *The Little Homeopapthic Physician*, Philadelphia, Boericke & Tapel, 1961.

23. Hand, Robert: *Planets In Transit*, Para Research, Gloucester, Massachusetts, 1976.

24. Harmon, J. Merrill: *Complete Astro-Medical Index*, Astro- Analytics Publications, Van Nuys, California, 1979.

25. Harvey, Ronald: *Mind & Body In Astrology*, L.N. Fowler & Co., Ltd., Essex, England, 1983.

26. Heindel, Max and Heindel, Augusta Foss: *Astro-Diagnosis A Guide to Healing*, The Rosicrucian Fellowship, Oceanside, California, 1973.

27. Hutcheon, Roger: *Planetary Pictures In Declination*, A.T.S. Press, Cambridge, Mass, 1976.

28. Jansky, Robert Carl: *Astrology Nutrition & Health*, Para Research, Rockport, Massachusetts, 1977.

29. Jansky, Robert C.: *Essays In Medical Astrology*, Astro-Analytics Publications, Van Nuys, California, 1980.

30. Jansky, Robert Carl: *Introduction To Holistic Medical Astrology,* American Federation of Astrologers, Inc., Tempe, Arizona, 1983.

31. Jansky, Robert C.: *Modern Medical Astrology*, Astro-Analytics Publications, Van Nuys, California, 1978.

32. Kares, Kasandra: *Encyclopedia Of Natural Remedies*, Astro-Analytics Publications, Van Nuys, California 1978.

33. Lineman, Rose: *Eclipse Interpretation Manual*, American Federation of Astrologers, Inc., Tempe, Arizona, 1986.

34. Mann, A.T.: *Astrology And The Art Of Healing*, Unwin Paperbacks, London, England, 1989.

35. Millard, Margaret: *Casenotes Of A Medical Astrologer*, Samuel Weiser, Inc., New York, New York, 1980.

36. Mindell, Earl: *Earl Mindell's Vitamin Bible*, Warner Books, New York, New York, 1979.

37. Munkasey, Michael: *Midpoints Unleasihing The Power Of The Planets*, ACS Publications, San Diego, CA, 1991.

38. Nauman, Eileen: *Medical Astrology*, Blue Turtle Publishing, Cottonwood, AZ, 1993.

39. Panos, M.D. Maesimund B. and Heimlich, Jane: *Homeopathic Medicine At Home,* G.P. Putnam's Sons, New York, 1980.

40. Pelletier, Robert: *Planets In Aspect*, Para Research, Inc., Gloucester, Massachusetts, 1974.

41. Rodale, J.I., and Staff: *Complete Book Of Minerals For Health*, Rodale

Books, Inc., Emmaus, PA, 1972.

42. Ridder-Patrick, Jan: *A Handbook Of Medical Astrology*, Arkana, London, England, 1990.

43. Rosenberg, Harold and A.N. Feldzamen: *The Doctor's Book Of Vitamin Therapy*, G.P. Putman's Sons, New York, New York, 1974.

44. Rothenberg, Robert E.: *Medical Dictionary And Health Manual*, New American Library, Inc., New York, New York, 1982.

45. Schifferes, Julius J.: *The Family Medical Encyclopaedia*, Pocket Books, New York, New York, 1977.

46. Starck, Marcia: *Atrology Key To Holistic Health.* Seek-It Publications, Birmingham, Michigan, 1982.

Glossary Bibliography

Medical Dictionary And Health Manual Fourth Revised Edition by Robert E. Rothenberg, M.D., F.A.C.S., New American Library, New York, New York, 1982.

Dorland's Illustrated Medical Dictionary Twenty-Sixth Edition, W.B. Saunders Company, Philadelphia, 1985.